VOICES

Leading on Purpose
*Intentionality and Teaming
in Congregational Life*

Eric Burtness

Augsburg Fortress

Minneapolis

This book is dedicated to Marilyn
who gives purpose and meaning to every breath of my life.

To our wonderful children: Amy, Matthew, John, Alex, and Laura
who have incredible gifts and abilities that they offer to God.

And to the people of St. Matthew
who have tolerated my mistakes, celebrated our successes,
and joined me on a significant journey toward the heart of God.

Leading on Purpose
Intentionality and Teaming in Congregational Life

Copyright © 2004 Augsburg Fortress. All rights reserved. Except for brief quotations in critical articles or reviews, no part of this book may be reproduced without prior written permission from the publisher. Write to: Permissions, Augsburg Fortress, Box 1209, Minneapolis, MN 55440.

Scripture quotations unless otherwise noted are from the New Revised Standard Version Bible, copyright © 1989 Division of Christian Education of the National Council of Churches of Christ in the United States of America. Used by permission.

The Concentric Circles and Baseball Diamond illustrations are from *The Purpose-Driven® Church* written by Rick Warren, pastor of Saddleback Church in Lake Forest, California, and author of the New York Times best-seller *The Purpose-Driven® Life*. Copyright © 1995 by Rick Warren. They are used with the permission of Purpose-Driven Ministries (www.purposedriven.com). All rights reserved.

Cover photo: © Royalty-Free/CORBIS

The paper used in this publication meets the minimum requirements of American National Standard for Information Sciences—Permanence of Paper for Printed Library Materials, ANSI Z329.48-1984.

Library of Congress Cataloging-in-Publication Data
Burtness, Eric, 1955–
   Leading on purpose : intentionality and teaming in congregational life / Eric Burtness.
    p. cm.
   Includes bibliographical references.
   ISBN 0-8066-5174-1 (alk. paper)
   1. Christian leadership. 2. Pastoral theology. I. Title.
   BV652.1.B865 2004
   253—dc22

                    2004018326

Manufactured in the U.S.A.   ISBN 0-8066-5174-1

08   07   06   05   04   2   3   4   5   6   7   8   9   10

Contents

CONCORDIA UNIVERSITY LIBRARY
PORTLAND, OR 97211

Foreword

As I read this book, my biggest frustration is that I'm forty-seven years old and not twenty-seven. But it's not too late for any of us, pastors or lay leaders in the church, to go about our calling more effectively, with greater fire in our bellies and a firmer commitment in our hearts. Pastor Eric Burtness, with the collected insights and experiences of other pastors and congregations and of experts in church health and growth, has compiled a highly practical guide that will inspire, encourage, and take you through concrete steps of transformation.

Back in the early '90s, as Eric and I served together as Associate Pastors at Bethlehem Lutheran in Minneapolis, we were teaching, preaching, and running ourselves ragged leading programs for couples, families, children, and youth. People seemed happy with the ministry, and the pews were still partially filled, but the membership numbers had quietly plateaued. I began to wonder, "Where am I leading people? I'm working hard, and doing what I was taught to do in seminary, but how are we changing the hearts of people, and what difference is this church making in the world?" I began to sense a "holy discontent," but wasn't sure how to make the changes needed, in my own heart, and then in the congregation I served.

I attended hosts of seminars and continuing education events seeking the answer. I came home with notebooks full of new program ideas I felt compelled to implement, but nothing was ever comprehensive enough, biblical enough, life-changing enough, or frankly simple enough to change my DNA for ministry. Sound at all familiar?

Now, years later, having sought to implement much of what I learned through Rick Warren and the Purpose-Driven approach, as well as from the smorgasbord of books that has come out from fine pastors such as Michael Foss, Dan Southerland, Walt Kallestad,

Leith Anderson, and dozens of others, we are all better equipped to help our congregations make the move from membership to discipleship, from committees to ministry teams, and from adult education that is informational to small groups that are transformational.

In this little book, Eric Burtness has taken "the best of" from much of this literature and put it into a very useable format that can assist any local parish pastor or leader in positive and permanent change. As I read his advice to help the reader process questions like, "Why does our church exist?" and "What is our purpose?" and his suggestions of hands-on ways to engage, empower, and equip people for ministry, I found myself taking notes. Eric offers ideas that can work in any congregation and other resources you can draw from, and his own website (www.leadingonpurpose.org) gives you a bushel of helpful tools.

Eric interprets and "legitimizes" for Lutherans Rick Warren's approach to ministry for all who believed that nothing good could come out of southern California. He convincingly points out that Warren's five purposes are not Baptist but clearly biblical. They are even found in our baptismal liturgy and our ELCA constitution. For all who still believe that being Purpose-Driven somehow doesn't fit our theology, it's time to get the baby back in the bathwater and open our minds and hearts to the wisdom and common-sense strategies that are helping churches across the country reclaim their sense of purpose for the sake of the gospel.

Our parishioners are not-so-patiently waiting for our church to catch the wave and be lit on fire once again with a renewed sense of mission. We want that to happen within the context of our theology and without having to let go of our liturgical tradition. This is possible! Many have done it or are seeking to do it—in congregations that still have pews, stained glass windows, organs, and altar guilds. The testimonies you will read in this book attest to that. Swedes and Germans, Somalians and Laotians, in Lutheran congregations are finding in this new paradigm for ministry a way to revitalize our churches and live out our baptismal calling with greater intentionality and integrity.

As I now bring many of these ideas to the third congregation in which I've implemented a Purpose-Driven approach, I guarantee that you will find in these pages a model for ministry that is life-giving for both you as leader and the people in your congregation.

May God bless your faithful and diligent work and give you patience and boldness as you seek to lead the people of God in such a time as this.

Pastor Tania Haber
Westwood Lutheran Church
St. Louis Park, Minnesota

Introduction

"Nothing seems to work anymore."

I was talking with Bob at a conference. He has been the pastor at Joyful Servant, an ELCA mission congregation, for the past eight years. The congregation had grown for the first several years, but once worship attendance reached an average of eighty about four years ago, everything began to plateau.

"I go home tired and frustrated every evening. I preach every Sunday, teach confirmation, lead the adult forum, visit the sick and homebound, make sure there are enough people on our nine committees, and attend every church function and activity. But nobody seems interested in taking any leadership; they rely on me to do it all. We have trouble getting Sunday school teachers and committee members, nobody wants to serve on the church council, and our choir continues to dwindle. I'm tired, I'm frustrated, and nothing I do seems to energize anyone to do anything. The congregation is fairly new, but people don't know what they want from their church, what they want from me, and most important, nobody knows what God is calling us to do."

Bob and his congregation are suffering from a lack of purpose and vision. Like many Lutheran congregations, people come occasionally to worship, hear a nice theological talk, and sing some fairly decent hymns or songs. They go home with a little something to think about, but without any direction or guidance about how it might make a difference in their lives on Monday morning. Things are "just fine" at Joyful Servant, but there is little joy, little serving, and a lot of ambivalence.

"I wish I knew something that could make a difference in my congregation," Bob said, "because nothing seems to work anymore."

Pastors Andy Romstad and Dennis Tollefson serve at Cambridge Lutheran Church in Cambridge, Minnesota. Cambridge is a small town north of Minneapolis. There had been struggles within the congregation between the mid-eighties and the mid-nineties, and the life of the congregation had become deflated and complacent. When Andy and Dennis started several years ago as a vibrant pastoral team, they began to work with committed members of the congregation to dream of new ways to do ministry that would transform the lives of the people and engage, empower, and equip them for ministry.

"We decided we wanted to commit ourselves to do whatever God is blessing, and to allow the Holy Spirit to work in and through us," Dennis said. As a vision caster, Dennis needed Andy, a strategist and implementer, to bring those visions to reality. Cambridge Lutheran has begun to be transformed. "We became fully committed to making Cambridge Lutheran a place where people would be encouraged to invite their friends to be inspired in worship, integrated into fellowship, involved in ministry, and increased in discipleship," Andy said.

When they realized through a Percept* survey that 60 percent of their community was unchurched, they immersed themselves in prayer, Bible study, workshops, reading, and meetings with the leadership of the congregation. Together, they discerned what God wanted them to be doing.

In the past two years, worship attendance has grown by 37 percent. An additional worship service has been added. Eighteen adults were baptized in one year. Instead of ministry being limited to pastoral time and energy, it is now shared and developed with more and more people. An additional Sunday school program, Promise Land, was added to target children from an unchurched background. People have come out of the woodwork to become involved in ministry. More and more people are giving of themselves for significant

*Contact Percept at (800)442-8277 for a "map" and "compass" of your demographic area. Your synod office is also a resource for this demographic survey of your area.

ministry; some people "work" at church as much as twenty to thirty hours each week.

"I'm sixty-five," Dennis said, "and I've never been more fulfilled in ministry. I know I'm doing what God wants me to be doing, and I'm having the time of my life. It's working!"

What's the difference between Joyful Servant and Cambridge Lutheran?

Cambridge Lutheran has discovered and implemented the purpose for which God calls, gathers, enlightens, and sanctifies the body of Christ. The congregation has focused on the Great Commandment and the Great Commission and on the purpose that God has for God's people and Christ's church.

That's what this book is about. And as each chapter unfolds you'll see specific ways in which your congregation can develop Great Commandment and Great Commission ministries that can transform your congregation's ministry to celebrate God's presence in worship, demonstrate God's love through ministry, communicate God's Word through evangelism, incorporate God's family through fellowship, and educate God's people through discipleship.

1

The Purpose-Driven Phenomenon

There's a new wave that is being caught by many churches across the country and throughout the world. It's a new wave based on Rick Warren's *The Purpose-Driven Church: Growth without Compromising Your Message and Mission*.[1] In the introductory chapter Warren writes, "Surfing is the art of riding waves that God builds. God makes the waves; surfers just ride them. If the waves aren't there, you just don't surf that day! On the other hand, when surfers see a good wave, they make the most of it, even if that means surfing in the middle of a storm."[2] It's not about building a wave or manufacturing a new program; it's realizing that it's only God who can make a church grow, and it's only God who can breathe new life into old bones.

The model of church life set out in this book is a structure for ministry. This is a book for pastors and church leaders to help you design a structure for ministry that enlightens the mind, engages the heart, and empowers the will of the people who gather on Sunday morning for worship and then serve God throughout the week. It's a book that is based on Scripture and implements it in specific ways to transform congregational life. It's a book that can be used in large and small, rural and urban, new and old congregations. It's not a new program that will fade with time, but it is a structure that will transform the spiritual DNA of your congregation. It's not a book of *theology*; you already have a theological base that drives the ministry of your congregation. It's a book about taking your theological base and structuring it into a vital, life-changing ministry.

Much of this book will be a Lutheran adaptation of the principles set forth in Warren's *The Purpose-Driven Church* and *The Purpose-Driven Life.*[3] These books have enjoyed tremendous popularity around the country, but many find they need to be adapted to fit in a Lutheran setting. Some people, when reading through *The Purpose-Driven Church*, find the emphasis on numbers to be distracting, the theology to be more driven by "decision" than by grace, and too much emphasis on *what we do* rather than on *what God has done*. Some of that criticism may be justified.

When our staff and congregation board read *The Purpose-Driven Church*, I encouraged them to identify what rang true in their ears and to disregard (for a moment, at least!) portions with which they disagreed. Some people underlined portions with two markers, one color to identify what would work for them and another color where they found disagreement. Not everything in either book works for all Lutherans, but I'm convinced that it's a structure for ministry that can transform lives, churches, teaching, and preaching, and can deepen one's growth as a disciple of Jesus Christ.

What Drives Your Church?

The first step is to realize that all churches are driven by *something*. Some churches are driven by tradition. When I was called as an associate pastor to one congregation to work with youth, I quickly found that there were many traditions. On my first Sunday there, a gentleman came up to me at the coffee hour. "Eric," he said, "it's good to have you here. Just remember, though, that we have many traditions in our youth program that are important to many people." As he concluded our short conversation, he looked over his glasses and said, "Don't try to change anything," and walked away.

Other churches are driven by the personality of the pastor, who has usually been there long enough to have pictures of the pastor and pastor's spouse prominently displayed in the Fellowship Hall. Other churches are driven by constant talk of money, giving, building, and stewardship. Other churches are driven by programs such as social ministry, outreach, youth, or well-developed ministries aimed at specific groups.

But think of what a church would look like that was built around the biblical purposes set forth in the Great Commandment and the Great Commission:

> You shall love the Lord your God with all your heart, and with all your soul, and with all your mind. This is the greatest and first commandment. And a second is like it: You shall love your neighbor as yourself. (Matthew 22:37-39)
>
> Go therefore and make disciples of all nations, baptizing them in the name of the Father and of the Son and of the Holy Spirit, and teaching them to obey everything that I have commanded you. (Matthew 28:19-20)

Those verses set forth the five purposes of the church.

- *Love the Lord your God* is worship, as we celebrate God's presence in worship.
- *Love your neighbor as yourself* is ministry, as we demonstrate God's love through ministry.
- *Go and make disciples* is evangelism, as we communicate God's Word through evangelism.
- *Baptizing them* is fellowship, as we incorporate God's family through fellowship.
- *Teaching them* is discipleship, as we educate God's people through discipleship.[4]

Balancing these five purposes is at the heart of the congregational structure of developing ministries that focus on worship, ministry, evangelism, fellowship, and discipleship. Pastors and leaders of the congregation should struggle with the question of what they want people in the community to know about Jesus, how they can best accomplish this, and what they want them to experience when they come to worship. Rick Warren writes, "Nothing discourages a church more than not knowing why it exists. On the other hand, the quickest way to reinvigorate a plateaued or declining church is to reclaim God's purpose for it and help the members understand the great tasks the church has been given by Christ."[5]

Over ten years ago William Easum listed several changes that were happening in mainline churches and that alarmed many church leaders at the time. We've seen Easum's changes confirmed in the changing culture of church life in this new century. Those changes included declining membership, declining Sunday school, declining mission programs and financial support, biblical illiteracy, fewer teenagers in attendance, and the increasing age of members, which means that within twenty-five years the majority of our current membership will no longer be able to attend worship because of their age. More than ten years ago he wrote that 80 percent of the churches in North America are plateaued or in decline.[6] Those dire predictions have become a reality in our church. Part of the reason for this continuing decline is that we've lost a sense of our purpose; we've continued to do things the way we've always done them, only it isn't working anymore. One answer to the malaise and ambivalence in our churches today is to passionately rediscover the biblical purposes that God has set forth in the Great Commission and the Great Commandment.

How might your congregation be different if members had a specific process through which they could develop spiritual maturity? What if you had defined discipleship paths that led to deeper commitment on a variety of levels? What if people could become engaged, empowered, and equipped for ministry? What if your congregation grew into a place of learning, growth, teaching, and equipping? What if more and more people were Christlike in their character, convictions, and conduct? Rick Warren suggests these things can be done by striving to develop three goals:

- Raise each member's level of commitment to Christ, to the congregation, and to spiritual growth. Boldly ask for, and expect, such a commitment.

- Help people develop spiritual growth habits, especially the four basic spiritual habits of Bible study, prayer, generous giving and sharing, and fellowship with other Christians.

- Build a balanced Christian Education ministry based on the five building blocks of spiritual maturity—knowledge, perspective, conviction, skills, and character.

In developing those five building blocks, ask these five questions:

Are people learning the content and message of the Bible?

Are people seeing themselves, other people, and life more clearly from God's perspective?

Are people's values becoming more aligned with God's values?

Are people becoming more skilled in serving God?

Are people becoming more like Christ?[7]

Questions for Discussion

1. What is the mission, vision, or purpose statement of your congregation? How well and how specifically is your congregation accomplishing it?

2. Which one of the five purposes of the church (worship, evangelism, fellowship, discipleship, and ministry) is the strongest in your congregation? Which is the weakest?

3. If you could have an equal balance among each of the purposes, what might your church look like? What changes might need to be made?

2

Intentionality
and Leading on Purpose

One day, when Alice was walking along, she came to a fork in the road. While she was pondering where to go, she saw the Cheshire Cat in a tree. Alice asked the Cat, "'Would you tell me, please, which way I ought to go from here?' 'That depends a good deal on where you want to get to,' said the Cat. 'I don't much care where—' said Alice. 'Then it doesn't matter which way you go,' said the Cat." [1]

How many churches could be characterized that way?

What kind of difference would it make if your congregation knew the path that God was calling them to take and could structure their ministries to accomplish the church's five purposes of evangelism, worship, fellowship, discipleship, and ministry?

Our Liturgies

When children are brought to the baptismal font, we use these five purposes of the church. The pastor begins by saying, "... By water and the Holy Spirit we are made members of the Church" (fellowship). Parents make this promise: "... You should, therefore, faithfully bring them to the services of God's house" (worship) and "provide for their instruction in the Christian faith" (discipleship). In the baptismal prayer the pastor says, "in obedience to [our Lord's] command, we make disciples of all nations, baptizing them in the name of the Father, and of the Son, and of the Holy Spirit" (evangelism). As the child is welcomed, the pastor says, "Through Baptism God has made these new sisters and brothers members of the priesthood we all share in Christ Jesus" (ministry).[2]

Those five purposes are also clearly stated when children grow to the age of confirmation and they are asked, "You have made public profession of your faith. Do you intend to continue in the covenant God made with you in Holy Baptism:

to live among God's faithful people, (fellowship)

to hear his Word and share in his supper, (worship)

to proclaim the good news of God in Christ through word and deed, (evangelism)

to serve all people, following the example of our Lord Jesus, (ministry)

and to strive for justice and peace in all the earth?"[3] (discipleship)

These five purposes are also in each congregation's Constitution. See C4.02, "To participate in God's mission, this congregation shall":

a. Worship God in proclamation of the Word and administration of the sacraments . . . (worship)

b. Carry out Christ's Great Commission . . . (evangelism)

c. Serve in response to God's love . . . (ministry)

d. Nurture its members in the Word of God . . . (discipleship)

e. Manifest the unity given to the people of God by living together in the love of Christ. . . (fellowship).

Those five purposes can also be seen in the High Priestly Prayer in John 17, in which Jesus prays for his disciples' ministry on the earth once he leaves them. The early church modeled these purposes in Acts 2:41-47, and Paul modeled these five purposes in Ephesians 4:11-16. Take some time to read through these passages, and circle the words that have to do with worship, evangelism, fellowship, discipleship, and ministry.

A New Model of Ministry

In the January 2004 issue of *The Lutheran*, Julie Sevig quoted Kenneth Inskeep, Director of the ELCA Department for Research and Evaluation, who said, "We need a model of what it means to do *Lutheran* ministry." The Purpose-Driven model is one that incorporates our Baptism liturgy, confirmation liturgy, and constitutions and is thoroughly biblical. The problem is that we just haven't done it!

Dave Waseman serves Christus Victor Lutheran Church in an affluent high-growth county just outside the beltway around Washington, DC. Dave has worked with the Purpose-Driven model in his congregation because of his conviction that "it's a back-to-basics moment in the life of the Lutheran church, an apostolic moment."

When Dave read through *The Purpose-Driven Church* with the leaders of his congregation, he also asked them to read Eric Gritsch's *Fortress Introduction to Lutheranism*. It's there that Gritsch writes, "The church as the body of Christ has a mission to the world: to baptize and make disciples of those who follow Jesus. . . . Worship is the key for formation for mission."[4] Gritsch asks about the relationship of good works to faith and writes, "The Bible provides a clear though surprising answer: good works are not done to appease God's wrath toward sinners, they are done to serve the neighbor in need."[5] The five purposes of the church are captured in Gritsch's words about the body of Christ.

As a second-career seminary graduate, Dave realized that he was prepared in seminary for preaching, worship, and visiting, but not for planning budgets, stewardship, or managing the church office. He also felt unprepared for evangelism and outreach. Dave's experience reflects the similar findings of a recent ChurchScan survey of 618 ELCA pastors in their first three years of ordained ministry.[6]

"We're at a critical Acts 2 moment in our church," Dave said, referring to the Day of Pentecost in the early church. "Without purpose and direction, we're adrift with great theology but no way to get it across to our people."

Concentric Circles of Commitment

One of the central points of *The Purpose-Driven Church* is recognizing that all churches have five concentric circles of commitment, starting with the community that knows virtually nothing about the church and moving inward to the core who are the key leaders and servants within the church. The church *cannot exist* without the core, and the church *exists* for the purpose of developing a specific path to eventually bring the community into the core. Developing specific strategies to feed, nurture, and lead the congregation through these circles is an important part of leading on purpose.

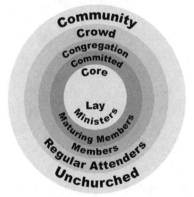

The community includes the unchurched people who live within driving distance of your church. Some of these people are totally unreceptive, some are somewhat receptive, some are very receptive, and some may even be lapsed Lutherans who are not a part of any church. The main question that people in the community are asking about your church is, "What is that church like?"

The crowd includes people who attend at least occasionally during the year. Sometimes referred to as "C & E" Christians (Christmas and Easter attenders), people in "the crowd" have at least a minor commitment to show up for occasional worship, much like the crowd of 5,000 people whom Jesus fed with five loaves and two fish. Jesus shared the truth about God with them without shaming them just because they weren't fully devoted followers. The main question that people in the crowd are asking about your church is, "What's here for me?" They ask the question of a consumer.

The congregation is the easiest circle to identify, because these are the people who are actually on the membership rolls of your congregation. These are the people to whom most ministry is directed. The main question that people in the congregation are asking is, "What should I be doing?"

The committed includes the members of the congregation who are growing toward spiritual maturity. They have made a commitment to worship, study, prayer, and giving, and they practice the habits necessary for spiritual growth. The main question that committed members are asking is, "Where else can I be involved?"

The core consists of those from the ranks of the committed who have made a commitment to being a ministry leader in your congregation. They are the ones who put their God-given gifts to work in a particular area of ministry in the church. The core is usually less than 5 percent of the total membership of your congregation. Their main question is, "How can our church serve others?"

The major question that congregational leadership should be asking is, "Do we have a specific discipleship process through which we can reach out to the community, bring them into the core, and then send them out to reach out to others in the community?"

A Discipleship Process

Another well-known "picture" of the discipleship process is the baseball diamond from Saddleback Church. It's a picture of how the community moves through a series of steps and classes in which people can learn discipleship habits that help them to grow into fully devoted followers who then move out again to those in the community.

This process begins with reviewing what you do in your new member classes. The new member class will determine how those new members will function in the congregation for years to come. When I used to teach new member classes in previous churches, I used to teach *information-based* classes. I would run all new members through a six- to eight-week new member class in which we'd go through the fundamentals of Lutheranism, the Small Catechism, and Lutheran church history. It was almost a Lutheran indoctrination class with lots of good information.

What I found, however, is that when people joined the congregation, they knew a lot about what it meant to be Lutheran, but I hadn't prepared them for a life of discipleship, learning, growth, and commitment. People who joined had good "head" knowledge, but their hearts and hands were not engaged, since enduring my Lutheran lectures was the main goal of the class!

Now, at St. Matthew, the goal of our new member class is not *indoctrination* but *incorporation*. Our goal is to provide an opportunity for people to become engaged in some form of ministry or service. We still provide a lot of written material about what it means to be Lutheran, but the major focus is getting people involved and engaged in some kind of ministry. When we accept new members on a Sunday morning, we tell some brief "fun facts" about each one, and we also name the specific congregational ministry to which they've committed themselves. This high-commitment new member process clearly shows that we're interested in growing disciples of Jesus Christ and not just adding members to our congregation.

The image of a baseball diamond has been used by many congregations as an image of "moving people around the bases" in designing specific discipleship paths. *First base* is the new member class, where people in the community are brought into the congregation through a commitment to membership. Remember that the best time for a person to decide if a church is right for them is before they join, and not after.

Second base is a commitment to spiritual maturity in which a congregation can offer a class that helps people develop spiritual habits of worship, prayer, Bible reading, and devotional life.

Third base is a commitment to ministry. A congregation might offer a class like SHAPE,[7] LifeKeys,[8] or other Spiritual Gift inventories. The goal of these inventories is to identify where people have a passion for ministry and then provide an opportunity for them to engage in meaningful ministry. This will be explored in the next chapter and is explained much more fully at www.leadingonpurpose.org.

Home plate is where people make a significant commitment to some kind of life-changing mission. While third base represents a *ministry in the church*, home plate represents a *mission in the world*. People who are fully devoted followers of Jesus Christ need to have both.

The baseball diamond has worked for many congregations for designing a discipleship process through which people can become fully devoted followers of Jesus Christ. For some, however, the baseball diamond is too "sports-oriented" and too linear.

At Bethlehem Lutheran in south Minneapolis (a fully developed Purpose-Driven church) they use a STAR design, based on *Starting* (first base), *Transforming* (second base), *Affirming* (third base) and *Reaching* (home plate).

At St. Matthew we use a building block analogy (ABCs) of building lives of discipleship through the steps of *Accepting* God's Call to Membership, *Building* Spiritual Habits, *Confirming* Your SHAPE, and *Serving* God's World. This building block analogy has greatly assisted us in structuring our ministry so that people can grow in their lives of discipleship and commitment.

But how do you go about engaging people in such a process? What compelling reason can you give so that people will want to grow deeper in their discipleship and live lives of service? That's what we'll talk about in the next chapter.

Questions for Discussion

1. Were you surprised that the purposes of worship, evangelism, fellowship, discipleship, and ministry could be found in our liturgies and constitution? What did you find when you looked at John 17:1-28 and Acts 2:41-47?

2. What was most helpful about the concentric circles of commitment? What was least helpful? Does your congregation have specific paths through which those in the community can eventually become a part of the core?

3. What does your congregation do during the new member process? In what specific ways can new members can become fully devoted followers of Jesus Christ? How are they presently told those ways?

4. What might your congregation look like in five years if you could develop specific discipleship paths? What are the barriers to developing discipleship paths in your congregation? How might those barriers be overcome?

3

Congregational Engagement: Getting the Order Right

Nita grew up in a large family that always cared for people in need. She felt comfortable with that form of ministry, but she never really directed her heart in any disciplined ministry. One day Beth, a friend who was struggling through her chemotherapy treatments, received a prayer shawl from a friend. Beth was very touched with this gift, and though she did not knit or crochet, she called Nita and said, "Nita, you have to come and see this gift, *and* you have to do it at St. Matthew. You just won't believe it! It's wonderful, soft, beautiful, and it simply has to be done at St. Matthew."

Nita was hooked from the moment she saw it. She immediately started to organize the process to start a congregational ministry team of prayer shawl knitters. She started working on our congregation's "Twelve Steps to Starting a Ministry Team," developed a mission statement, and by the day's end she had a basic plan in her head and a mental list of crafters, knitters, and crocheters.

The design for the shawls was to knit three, purl three, and to pray to the Father, Son, and Holy Spirit the whole time the shawl was being knit. When she took the proposal to the Stephen Ministers' group, she immediately had three willing knitters, three who were willing to learn to knit, and a thirty-dollar contribution for seed money. Nita knew that the combination of the threes was God's stamp of approval for her ministry.

One hundred three prayer shawls have been given to members of our congregation in the past nine months—more than three each week. Some have gone to young mothers, some to people facing crisis, and some to people in nursing homes. Several people have been buried with their prayer shawls draping their bodies. It is a significant ministry that began when God knocked on the door of Nita's heart. It wasn't the idea of one of the pastors, it didn't require budget or Board approval, and the thirty-five people who knit the shawls are engaged in a meaningful ministry that touches hearts and changes lives. Nita is able to hear and experience God more than ever in her daily life and is blessed every time she is involved in giving someone a shawl. She now can pray with strangers and those she loves without a second thought. You can read some of her "stories of the shawls" at www.leadingonpurpose.org.

Fully Devoted Followers

While the storm raged, the disciples saw what they believed to be a ghost, until they realized that it was Jesus. Peter, still not convinced that it was Jesus, tested him by asking him to walk on the water. Jesus simply invited him to take a step toward him. As Peter did, he sank into the water. We often think that this was just another example of Peter's enthusiasm that led to failure. The ones who really failed, however, were the eleven disciples who stayed in the comfort of the boat, waiting to see what would happen to Peter.[1]

I'd take one Peter over the other eleven any day of the week.

As Michael Slaughter has written, "I don't want to lead a megachurch of people who come together to be inspired to live status-quo lives peppered with Judeo-Christian values. I want to empower radical followers of Jesus."[2]

Nita was not just a knitter. Through her prayer shawl ministry she had become more fully engaged in a significant ministry that deepened her discipleship, ministered to others, and drew her closer to the heart of God.

A Process of Engagement

The Gallup Organization has done some groundbreaking work in congregational engagement. They found that people who are engaged in congregational life are three and a half times more likely to say that they are strongly satisfied with their lives than disengaged people. Engaged people are more than three times as likely to invite someone to visit their congregation, and they spend as many as three times as many hours each week taking part in community service compared with those who are not engaged. They also found that engaged members give 50 percent more money to their congregations than those who are not engaged and more than three times as much as those who are actively disengaged.

Gallup suggests that the evidence is clear: If you want to grow a spiritually healthy, vibrant, dynamic congregation, focus on increasing the engagement level of your members.

Nita was engaged. As more and more people become engaged in congregational life, their life satisfaction rises, their giving increases, their attendance rises, and they become fully devoted followers of Jesus Christ.

Satisfied Versus Loyal (Engaged) Members

One of the benefits of living in Oregon is that we don't pump our own gas. You can kill yourself in Oregon (doctor-assisted suicide is legal), but you can't pump your own gas. Figure out that one.

For five years I went to the local gas station, asked the attendant to fill the car, went inside to pay, and by the time I returned, my car was set to go. I was very satisfied. One day a change came at the local gas station. Under new management, I now had to ask for a fill and go inside to pay. The attendant wouldn't start to pump my gas until I paid inside, which meant that my car wasn't ready by the time I returned.

I wasn't angry, but I left that gas station and began to give my business to another one where they treated me like the first. I had been satisfied at the previous gas station, but I wasn't loyal, and my loyalties went elsewhere where my needs were met the way I wanted. I know that happens with gas stations and grocery stores. Does that ever happen in your congregation?

In the next two chapters we'll look at becoming engaged in the life of a congregation in a way that helps discover people's gifts for ministry in order to engage, empower, and equip them for ministry. When that happens, people become loyal members of your congregation. They're much more than just satisfied customers or consumers who move away when they perceive their "needs" are not being met; they're loyal and devoted followers of Jesus who are engaged in the ministry of your congregation.

Our Spiritual Climate

Gallup's research has found that 82 percent of the American public has an interest in spiritual growth and 86 percent say they believe in God. And while 80 percent of Americans believe that there is salvation only through Jesus Christ, 75 percent of the same people believe that other religions offer a true path to God.[3]

How is that possible?

One reason for this may be that most people are fundamentally biblically illiterate; they know *that* they believe, but they don't know *what* they believe. Gallup's statistics show that it's not that people *don't believe;* it's that they believe *just about anything!* In the cultural shift from Christendom to pluralism, people are trying to make sense of the exclusive claim of Jesus Christ in an inclusive context and culture.

Additionally, Gallup has identified three "gaps" in congregational life. First, there is an ethics gap, which is the difference between the way we would like to think of ourselves and the way we actually are. "Religion" is very popular in our country, but it does not engage or change people's lives in a way that one might expect. Many people believe, but their behavior doesn't reflect their beliefs; their faith has not engaged their lives. Second, there is a knowledge gap between what people say they believe and what they actually know about the Bible. Again, most of us know of the biblical illiteracy of many people in and around our congregations. Third, there is a growing gap between believers and unbelievers and a decoupling of faith and practice. Many people say they are believers, but they cannot be found in any church on Sunday morning.

All of this combines to give a tremendous breadth to American Christianity, but not much depth. Our values of relativism, pluralism, privatism, and hedonism combine with our busy lives and daily distractions to solidify the "disconnect" between what people say they believe and the way in which they live their lives.

On the other hand, there has never been a more opportune time for the church to reach out with the life-changing gospel of Jesus Christ to attract and empower our members and friends to be fully devoted followers of Jesus Christ. There has never been a time when leading on purpose is more important, nor has there been a time when what we are doing in our individual churches can reach more people. As Jesus said, the harvest is ripe, and he is waiting and looking for people who are willing to work toward the harvest.

Are you willing to work toward the harvest that our Lord is providing?

Most of our unchurched friends and neighbors pray. Most of them want deeper and more significant relationships, especially at a time when many of their relationships are breaking up. Just about every young family wants some kind of religious training for their children. Church members want to have their voices heard, and most pastors and church leaders are still held in relatively high esteem in their communities.

This is an incredible time to be the church. You can make the difference in someone's life not only now, but for an eternity. Your congregation's mission and ministry can engage, empower, and equip people for specific ministries in the places where they're gifted, rather than just where you need them. In that way you can build a process through which people become fully devoted followers of Jesus Christ.

There are three ways to build congregational engagement into your congregational mission and ministry.

First, focus on engagement before spiritual commitment. For many years I focused on increasing the spiritual commitment level of the people in the congregations I served. I used to think that if my focus was on the spiritual health and commitment of the congregation, that people would automatically become actively engaged in the congregation, spend more time serving, be more inviting toward others, and give more of their financial resources to support the congregation's ministry.

I was partly right, but for years it felt like I was spinning my wheels without making much progress. I should have followed Jesus' example. Jesus had four clearly distinct levels of commitment that corresponded to his follower's stage of spiritual commitment. He realized that no two people were at the same point in terms of commitment, engagement, and maturity. Jesus was a master of drawing people to the next level, much like the concentric levels of commitment in the previous chapter.

The first level was "Come and See" (John 1:39). During the early stages of Jesus' ministry he just wanted people to observe who he was and what he did. He answered a lot of questions that the multitude had about what it meant to follow him, but at this initial stage the goal was only observation.

The second level was "Follow Me" (Mark 1:17). This level included many "members" who were growing in their spiritual maturity and who learned personal disciplines of prayer and commitment. Those who followed Jesus gradually learned the critical transition from sincere converts to fully devoted followers.

The third level was "Come and Be" (Mark 3:14). By the time many people were following Jesus, he found it necessary to select twelve people to *be with him*. These were people who didn't only believe things *about* him but believed *in* him. Jesus allowed them to develop their own ministry as apprentices. He developed this four-fold training method: first, I do and you watch; second, we do together; third, you do and I'll applaud (or affirm); and fourth, you do and have someone else watch.

The fourth level was "Remain in Me and Go" (John 15; Matthew 28:19-20). In his final words to his disciples, Jesus gave them lessons on leadership, love, confidence, prayer, and obedience. "Abide in me, and you will bear much fruit. Apart from me you can do nothing" (John 15:5). Having trained his disciples, he left the future of the church in their hands. They were now fully engaged and devoted followers.

Can you see the same levels as the concentric circles of commitment from the previous chapter? Jesus reached out to the community and engaged them through different levels of commitment to become core, engaged followers. When he first called his disciples along the shores of the Sea of Galilee, he wasn't asking them to believe right off the bat. He was calling them to learn, grow, and mature in their faith so that they might become fully devoted and engaged followers.

We can learn something from that process as we reach out to our unbelieving communities and develop a process to bring them into the core.

Second, focus on discipleship, not membership. Many churches focus much of their time and energy on those who are members. Some conversations I've been a part of in previous years sound like a commercial for American Express: "Membership has its privileges." This gets played out in who votes at annual meetings, who gets the newsletter mailings, who gets the privilege of a church funeral, and who gets a lower price when planning a wedding. It even gets played out on church signs. I asked one person why the worship service times weren't printed on his church sign. His reply:

"The people who need to know already know. Those who don't know don't need to know."

Mike Foss preceded me as senior pastor at St. Matthew and now serves at Prince of Peace in Burnsville. His recent book, *Power Surge: Six Marks of Discipleship for a Changing Church* (Fortress Press), is a must-read in making the transition from membership to discipleship.

In his book he makes the distinction between membership and discipleship: "Membership is about getting; discipleship is about giving. Membership is about dues; discipleship is about stewardship. Membership is about belonging to a select group with its privileges and prerogatives; discipleship is about changing and shaping lives by the grace of God."[4]

It's difficult to make the transition from membership to discipleship, but if we are truly committed to reaching out to the community with the goal of building fully devoted followers of Jesus Christ, then the distinction between membership and discipleship gets a little fuzzy. However, the goal should always clearly be growth in discipleship, rather than increasing the numbers we can list on our annual parochial report.

An example of this is who gets to be married at church. At St. Matthew we get lots of requests for non-member weddings. We also live in the most unchurched state in the nation, where there are more people with no Christian memory than almost any other state. Many people here have never heard of lutefisk, they don't know that you eat ham and sweet potatoes on Easter Sunday, and they can't understand why the male pastors wear a dress when they come to their cousin's confirmation.

But some young couples want to have a wedding at church because it's important to Grandma. Instead of charging them three times the "member" rate, we have chosen to make some requirements of all couples seeking to get married at St. Matthew.

a. We charge all couples the same rate; no member "privileges." We only charge fees for personnel, and not a church fee.

b. We ask that all couples worship at St. Matthew at least six times in the four months prior to the wedding.

c. We require all couples to go through our three-session pre-marriage class, which introduces them to other couples in the same circumstance of life.

d. We ask the couple to meet with our wedding coordinator before the rehearsal to plan the details.

In that way, every couple has as many as twelve positive contacts with the church before their wedding takes place. What we've seen is that many of these couples start to worship on a regular basis after their wedding. If they have children, we've seen them have the child baptized and then register the child for Sunday school in future years.

If we had been focused only on membership, we would have missed the opportunity to invite people into discipleship. That's only one small example of how a congregation's focus can shift.

Mike Foss writes, "The move from membership to discipleship is not easy. Trying to change from the mind-set, values, and behavior patterns of any community is difficult at best and perilous at worst. But it can be done, over time and incrementally. It has happened before."[5]

Again, people need to be invited in, rather than shut out. If people are not invited in at the most basic levels, we miss the opportunity to engage them as fully devoted followers.

Third, focus on people's gifts, not the church's needs. Michael is an attorney who works with wills and estates. Since he had a financial background, he seemed to be a natural fit for our Board when we were looking for a Board treasurer. For four years Michael did a great job just where we needed him, and he served us well.

But in Michael's spare time he was reading books and listening to lectures on spiritual health and commitment. He traveled with me to Las Vegas to a meeting of the largest West Coast ELCA congregations, and he felt God calling him to switch his involvement from *where we needed him* to where he was *truly gifted to serve*—on our Spiritual Formation Ministry Team. Next year he will become the Board chair. Michael's real passion and his gift were the spiritual health and engagement of our congregation. While he served very well as treasurer, he has been "on fire" as a spiritual leader.

Far too many times we twist people's arms and try to get them to serve in places where we need them. But think of what your congregation would look like if people were serving in areas where they were truly gifted, and not just where they are needed. A person's secondary ministry is where they are needed, and that's normally where we fill spots with volunteers. But a person's primary ministry is where they are gifted, and when you match a person's giftedness with an opportunity for serving, real ministry begins to happen in incredible ways!

There are several resources available for your congregation to use in discovering that giftedness. *LifeKeys* is one of the best. It can help people better understand themselves, gain an appreciation for people around them, get in touch with God's purpose for themselves, and clarify where they may be best fit to serve within your congregation. You can find out more at www.LifeKeys.com or find the other assessments listed below at www.leadingonpurpose.org.

Saddleback Church's SHAPE program is also excellent. It involves an inventory that helps people identify their Spiritual gifts, Heart (passion), Abilities, Personality (through the Myers-Briggs Inventory), and Experience. Once people work to discover their SHAPE, they also find ways in which they can become much more fully engaged in congregational life.[6]

A third resource is an internet inventory (www.strengthsfinder.com) in a book published by Gallup called *Living Your Strengths: Discover Your God-Given Talents and Inspire Your Congregation and Community.*[7] Each book will give you a StrengthsFinder identification code that helps you through a process of gift discovery and then provides an extensive list of places where people can fulfill God's purpose in their lives. This resource could be beneficial for your congregation's staff or council and could begin the transformational process that we'll talk about in later chapters.

All of this, I believe, helps us realize that we need a revolutionary, paradigmatic change in our churches to help engage, empower, and equip people for meaningful ministry. People need a ministry in the church and a mission in the world, and for far too long the church has neglected the incredible ministry potential of people who sit in the pews each week. There's a sleeping giant out there, and our worship spaces are filled with people longing to give significantly of their time, their talents, and their treasures. When you lead on purpose, you catch the vision of unleashing this potential for ministry.

For church leaders and pastors, there isn't anything more exciting, more rewarding, and more significant than structuring your congregation's ministry around that vision.

How to do that is the topic of the next chapters.

Questions for Discussion

1. How (by what path) do new members of your congregation begin a process of engagement to becoming fully devoted followers of Jesus Christ? How do you publicize this path? What are the first steps you can take to construct such a path, if one doesn't exist?

2. Who appear to be some of the most engaged members in your congregation? Who are the disengaged members? What affects the levels of engagement?

3. What would your church look like if you focused on discipleship, not membership? What policies would have to change?

What kind of process could you set up to help people move through the process of Come and See, Follow Me, Come and Be, and Remain and Go?

4. If you dared to dream about something you could do at church that would utilize your gifts, talents, passion, abilities, and experience, what would that be? Is there an opportunity for you to use your gifts in that way? If not, what would you need to do to make those opportunities available?

4

Ministry Teams

Our heroes have often been cowboys.

It's the Lone Ranger, Spider Man, and the rugged individualist. It's the admiration we have for those who pull themselves up by their own bootstraps. It's the self-made woman. It's the guy who claws his way to the top. We respect the rugged individual and hold those who make it on their own in high esteem. And we admire and revere the pastor who is able to "do it all" with preaching, teaching, administrating, visiting, counseling, leading, chanting, and organizing everything that happens at church.

That is, however, until the pastor burns out, gets angry, leaves for another congregation, and repeats the same behavior all over again.

And the people of the local congregation lose the most.

The myth of the heroic leader is antithetical to a church that values and affirms the gifts of each and every person. It has been particularly damaging as a crippling delusion when people sometimes think that the pastor is the key person around which everything revolves in the life of a congregation.

In *Reclaiming the "L" Word*, Kelly Fryer writes:

Who started this?!? There is this crazy idea out there that somehow church "starts" when the pastor says so. Or that you can't have church if there's no pastor. If that were true, then all those churches out there who are "between" pastors or have a "part time" pastor or "share" a pastor or will never have a pastor . . . aren't real churches at all. And you and I both know that's not true. Where did this wacky idea come from?!? Well, I don't know. And I don't know why it continues to be this way in so many churches. But I know one thing for sure; it is not in the Bible.[1]

Recapturing the Biblical Notion of Teamwork

The biblical vision for pastoral leadership is clearly set out in Ephesians:

> The gifts he gave were that some would be apostles, some prophets, some evangelists, some pastors and teachers, to equip the saints for the work of ministry, for building up the body of Christ, until all of us come to the unity of the faith and of the knowledge of the Son of God, to maturity, to the measure of the full stature of Christ. (Ephesians 4:11-13)

Pastors are called to prepare people for the work of ministry, for unity, for knowledge, for maturity, and for growing toward the measure of the full stature of Christ. That's the vision and the direction for how pastors should spend their time. It's not about being a lone ranger; it's about engaging, empowering, and equipping people for their ministry in the church and for their mission in the world.

Again, we can use Jesus as a model. When Jesus started his ministry, he was very clear about the vision and direction of what he needed to do. In Luke 4:43 Jesus said, "I must proclaim the good news of the kingdom of God to the other cities also; for I was sent for this purpose." Jesus was very clear about the direction and purpose of his life, and it was to go forth from where he was and preach the good news.

But in order to do that, Jesus quickly knew that he needed to form a team. Immediately after Jesus stated his purpose he stood by the Sea of Galilee and watched Peter fishing. He got into Peter's boat, and taught the crowd from the boat. When he was finished teaching, he said to Peter, "Put out into the deep water and let down your nets for a catch" (Luke 5:4).

This was absurd advice to give a veteran fisherman like Peter. Peter knew that the sheltered, shallow coves were the best for fishing.

He also knew that fishing was best at night when the fish were feeding, rather than during the day. From an expert fisherman's perspective, there were many reasons not to put the nets out into the deep in the middle of the day. So Peter responded, "Master, we have worked all night long but have caught nothing" (Luke 5:5). Can you hear what Peter is saying? He's saying, "We've never done it that way before."

From this Bible verse we can conclude beyond any reasonable doubt that Peter was Lutheran. He said the famous Lutheran Seven Last Words: *We've never done it that way before.* Peter wanted to keep doing what was familiar and what would produce predictable results, even if those efforts produced predictable failure. He didn't want to step out and do something bold and different from the way that he had always been living his life.

Nonetheless, he said, "But if you say so, I will let down the nets." It was at that moment that Jesus wanted him as a part of his team. After the huge catch was hauled into the boat, Jesus said to Peter and James and John, "Do not be afraid; from now on you will be catching people" (Luke 5:10).

This was Jesus doing team ministry.

Jesus and Teams

Jesus was a team builder. He spent time alone in prayer, but most of his time during his public ministry was spent being surrounded with three distinct teams of people. Jesus closely surrounded himself with an Executive Team—Peter, James, and John. Peter was the lead fisherman of an entrepreneurial fishing team, and James and John were the sons of Zebedee, which means "sons of Thunder." They had worked together for some time before Jesus stood on the shores of the lake and called them to be his first disciples.

They were not only the first disciples whom Jesus called but also his closest confidants. The three of them were with Jesus through the heights and depths of his life—at the Mount of Transfiguration and at the Garden of Gethsemane. They were the ones that Jesus went to when life was rewarding, difficult, or challenging.

Beyond the Executive Team, Jesus surrounded himself with a Core Team, comprised of the twelve disciples. These are the ones who had left their friends and family to follow Jesus. Jesus traveled with them on dusty roads and in boats. He taught them and performed miracles with them at his side. Eventually he died for them and then passed on to them the task of continuing his gospel ministry.

The third team with which Jesus worked was a Missions Team. After he taught his disciples and sent them out, he also trained and taught another missions team of seventy people and sent them out in the same way. They went two by two into the neighboring towns to spread the good news to the surrounding villages of unbelievers (Luke 10). With the other teams, they became fully devoted followers.

Through these three teams, Jesus changed the world.

Maintenance and Mission, Committees and Teams

Is your congregation structured for maintenance and control, or is it structured to be a permission-giving culture in which ministry can flourish?

Imagine the following committee-laden congregation that is structured for maintenance and control. A church council has liaisons from each of the sixteen church committees, with a total council membership of twenty-four people. When it comes time to paint the women's bathroom, the WELCA (Women of the ELCA) committee presents a recommendation to the council to paint it mauve. The finance committee says there is a shortage of money, and it should be deferred until the next month. At the next meeting the property committee says they want to do a study on the color of the bathrooms and make a recommendation at the next council meeting. At the next month's council meeting the property committee recommends that the women's bathrooms should be painted taupe and the men's bathrooms should be painted latte. But the finance committee says that there still isn't enough money to paint all the bathrooms, so it should be deferred to the next council meeting. In the meantime, the WELCA committee gets so fed up that they decide not to bring any more recommendations to the council, and the bathroom remains unpainted.

At St. Matthew we are structured to have a streamlined Board, made up of four officers (president, vice-president, secretary, and treasurer) and five at-large members. Each of the five at-large members is assigned to one of the five purposes of the church: worship, evangelism, fellowship, discipleship, and ministry. These Board members are referred to as "Board champions." Board champions have a passion for a particular purpose, and their role is to network with all the ministry teams assigned to that particular purpose. We currently have more than fifty active ministry teams, each of which operates under one of the five purposes.

Board champions are not "liaisons" who need to attend every ministry team meeting, but they are to keep their ears tuned to what's happening in those ministry teams. In addition, at St. Matthew each program staff member is also assigned to a purpose, so these folks are referred to as the "staff resource persons." Their responsibilities are similar to that of the Board champion, and with the ministry team leader they operate as the Executive Team of each of the purposes.

Our congregation's Board only has five committees that do the maintenance work of the Board: personnel, stewardship, finance, long-range planning, and leadership development. Each of these five committees has a Board liaison who regularly attends the meetings, along with a staff person (who may serve on more than one committee). The committees do the maintenance work of the Board.

In this way, the Board governs, the staff administrates, the committees do maintenance, and the people do ministry through ministry teams. In smaller congregations, where there are fewer staff people, an active lay member can serve as a resource person for each of the five purposes and would then be a part of an Executive Team with the pastor and others.

Bill Easum describes attributes of ministry teams in his classic book *Sacred Cows Make Gourmet Burgers: Ministry Anytime Anywhere by Anyone*:

1. People closest to the ministry know what is best for that ministry.
2. Most people want to "own" their ministry and be free to contribute to its effectiveness.
3. Teamwork develops people better than individual roles or offices.[2]

Ministry teams consist of people wanting to do specific tasks in a team setting; they operate best in a culture with these core convictions:

1. In a permission-giving culture, *doing* ministry is more important than *controlling* who does ministry.
2. Ministry is more important than maintenance.
3. Those doing ministry should be able to make the decisions about the ministry, including decisions about spending available budget monies.

In *Power Surge* Mike Foss describes the difference between ministry teams and committees after a conference talk:

> At the end of my talk, a young woman stood to ask a question that I often hear: "I still don't get it," she said. "Just what is the difference between a ministry team and a committee?"
>
> "Well, let me ask you all a question," I replied. "You are all lay leaders in your congregations. So tell me, how many of you would be willing to serve on another committee?"

My question generated the response I expected—only those over age fifty-five raised their hands. As committed lay leaders, they wanted to serve their congregations in whatever way needed. As folks who had been around a while, they knew the frustration of working with a committee structure.

"For those of you who didn't raise your hands," I went on, "let me ask you why you didn't."

A young woman, who appeared to be in her mid-thirties, blurted out, "It's simple. Committees don't do anything! They just talk and talk and talk!"

Looking at her I asked, "But if you were asked to join a team of people to accomplish a specific goal that you cared about, in a given time period, would you do it?"

"In a heartbeat," she responded.

Turning to the woman who had asked the original question, I said, "That is the difference between a committee and a ministry team."[3]

Starting Ministry Teams

When starting a ministry team, consider asking the following.

1. Which of the five purposes of the church fits our ministry team? A ministry team begins with a ministry team leader, in coordination with the Board champion and the staff resource person. These three people should make up the core leadership of any ministry team. Communication may only be through e-mail or brief phone messages, or it may be necessary to meet to vision, plan, and coordinate the ministry. Beyond that, the ministry team may involve as many other people as it needs to get the ministry accomplished.

Since ministry teams grow out of a specific ministry need, there should be several convictions before even starting a ministry team.

- Ministry teams should not be started without a ministry team leader.
- Those doing the ministry should make the decisions about the ministry.

- Funds for the ministry shouldn't be raised outside the annual operating budget.
- Each ministry team should be theologically sound and in line with the mission, vision, and values of the congregation.
- Since ministry team leaders play such an important role in the congregation's overall ministry, a standard background check should be done on a ministry team leader before the ministry team begins to function.

As the ministry team's core leaders begin the germination of a ministry team, questions to be asked should include, "What is God calling us to do? What do we feel God is blessing? What will happen if we don't respond to God's call?"

The core leadership team should then discern which of the five purposes of the church is fulfilled with this ministry team. Is it to communicate God's Word through evangelism? Is it to celebrate God's presence in worship? Is it to incorporate God's family through fellowship? Is it to educate God's people through discipleship? Is it to demonstrate God's love through ministry?

You can probably already begin to categorize any ministry team or committee that is currently active in your congregation with one of these purposes.[4]

2. Which concentric circle of commitment does our ministry team target? A ministry team is much stronger in vision and direction if it identifies a specific target group, rather than trying to target both the community and the core at the same time.[5] This may be offensive to some, but it's important to remember that when Jesus sent out his disciples in Matthew 10:5-6 he sent them out with the "target" group of the lost sheep of the house of Israel. Paul targeted the Gentiles in his ministry. Peter targeted the Jewish converts. The clearer the focus on a target, the more effectively the ministry team can coordinate their efforts.

The core leaders of the ministry team should determine whether the team should target the *community* (occasional attenders at Christmas and Easter), the *crowd* (weekend attenders), the *congregation* (those committed to membership), the *committed* (those committed to spiritual maturity), or the *core* (those committed to ministry).

At St. Matthew we have a cars ministry team that accepts donated cars, fixes them up, and gives them away to needy people.[6] Each year about thirty-five cars are given away free of charge through a very well-organized process that identifies which people are in need. The target for the recipients is the *community*. However, the cars are often presented in a worship service (if the recipients are bold enough to come!) in which they often give testimony about the difficulty they have faced in their lives and how much difference this free car can make. It often brings tears to people's eyes when they hear about divorce, poverty, drugs, and abuse people face and the tremendous need they have for transportation. In this way, though the primary target is the community, the congregation and the committed are the secondary targets, as these testimonies often result in more cars or money from the *core* being donated to this ministry team.

3. How should our ministry team be configured? This is a question of effective strategy. What needs are being met with the ministry team? Are they primarily physical, spiritual, emotional, or intellectual? Will the ministry team provide meals for the homeless or develop internet teaching tools? Does it require spiritual maturity on the part of its members, or is it made up mostly of "doers" of a particular ministry?

The dream of a ministry team is placed in someone's heart long before a ministry team is brought together to develop that dream. Many ministry teams begin their germination after a conversation with a pastor or leader from the church. In a permission-giving culture, it's important to develop a ministry team to be fluid and agile, rather than getting bogged down in bureaucracy and buried in paperwork.

That's why it's important to coordinate ministry teams with a staff resource person and a Board champion in order to identify the kinds of roles and responsibilities needed to fill the ministry team. The issue is not control; it's coordination and cooperation.

It's important to define the categories of people needed on a ministry team. Skills in leadership, shepherding, administering, communicating, promoting, training, orienting, fellowship, and spiritual growth should be a part of each ministry team. A ministry team leader can't assume all of those responsibilities, but he or she can make sure that each one is addressed on the ministry team.

To identify people who most likely can be ministry team leaders, it's important to have the leaders be engaged members of the congregation. It's most helpful if the leader can complete some of the engagement resources mentioned in chapter 3, like LifeKeys, SHAPE, or the StrengthsFinder.[7] This will help enormously in the success and the configuration of the ministry team.

4. What kind of training and support is needed for the ministry team? This question is an important "functional" question related to internal mentoring, on-the-job training, or classes that are directed toward leading the growth of the ministry team. It also addresses the question of what is needed from the church in terms of rooms or space. Is it computer access or mailboxes for the ministry team? What kind of staff time is needed to support the ministry team? What kind of funding is required?

One important aspect of starting a ministry team is not to regularly raise funds for the ministry outside of the annual operating budget of the congregation. There may be occasional fundraisers, but if people start to designate their offering to the ministry of their choice, then the overall ministry of the congregation begins to suffer. This is, of course, something that requires careful consideration in your own setting.

In most settings, Board or council approval should not be required for starting a ministry team. If it doesn't require outside funding; if it fits within the vision, values, and mission of the congregation; and if it answers the questions above, the ministry team should only require coordination, not permission. A new ministry team might be "commissioned" at a Sunday morning worship service, when there is a description of the ministry team, the names of those involved, a mission statement of what drives the ministry team, and an invitation for others to become involved.

5. How will the ministry team communicate? Communication always takes more time than we think, but it is very important. Each ministry team should determine how to communicate with one another, with the staff, with the Board or council champion, and with the congregation. Part of the communication process is not only keeping lines of communication open but also providing a way to welcome others into the ministry team.

Testimonies are a particularly effective way to communicate what happens through the ministry team. A Sunday morning testimony can include stories of how hearts were touched and lives were changed through the ministry team. Part of the reason that faith communicators are failing to attract people and engage them is because stories are not being told of life-transformation that happens through the congregation's ministry. We'll talk more about this in the next chapter.

6. How will this ministry team grow? What is the ministry team's plan for the future? If it's true that each ministry team began with the dream that God placed in someone's heart, what is that dream? What will that dream look like two years from now, and what specific steps can be taken to accomplish that goal?

How will the team be led and shepherded, and what kind of mentoring relationship can be put in place to groom a new leader of the ministry team? A ministry team leader should always have an accomplice, either one who is prepared to lead the ministry in the near future or one who is able to start a new ministry team with another focus.

Ministry team leaders should operate with the philosophy of *planned obsolescence.* If a ministry team is based around the passion and personality of the ministry team leader, what happens if the leader moves? Ministry teams should never be led by lone-ranger types but by people who want to "work themselves out of a job" by teaching and training others. There should always be a mentoring process to bring others into leadership. See some examples of this at www.leadingonpurpose.org.

My personal mission statement for the congregation I serve is this: *to have a significant impact on the congregation's ministry in such a way that it won't be significantly affected if I leave, die, or retire.* That's planned obsolescence. I've seen too many congregations, youth ministries, and team ministries that revolve around the passion and personality of one of their leaders. That kind of lone-ranger ministry doesn't replicate itself, nor does it provide leadership training for others.

In the next chapter we will move on to talk about preaching to increase the commitment level of your congregation.

Questions for Discussion

1. Who is the primary leader in your congregation? What kind of teamwork do you have with your leadership? Is there shared responsibility in planning, outcomes, and recognition?

2. Is your congregation structured for maintenance and control or for ministry and mission? Is there cultural permission to start new ministry teams? If you're structured with a council system, would it make sense to be structured for ministry teams, and what would it take to have that happen?

3. What would be a good idea in your congregation for a new ministry team? What purpose would it serve, and which circle would it target?

4. What would it take if you were to support your pastor and church council to begin making some of these changes?

5

Preaching on Purpose

Preaching is one of the most personal things that a pastor does on a public stage. Suggesting a course of action for preaching is not done without some trepidation, but I offer this chapter as a conversion experience after having my preaching transformed over the past several years.

When I was trained at the seminary, I was prepared to proclaim the Word. I had the best teachers and received the best theological training available. In my first parishes I tried to proclaim the Word in the best way I knew how every time I preached. I preached a theology of the cross, not a theology of glory. I preached both law and gospel, and I put many hours into exegesis so I could come as close as possible to the meaning of the original text. My goal was to preach Jesus Christ, and him crucified. My goal was to be transparent. The preacher didn't matter; only Jesus did. And if Jesus didn't have to die for the sermon to be preached, then the sermon wasn't worth preaching.

But in those early years of preaching I don't think I changed anyone's life one single bit. I focused on proclamation, and sometimes a little exhortation, but I left the application portion of a sermon up to the listeners. Surely, I thought, they could easily figure out how my theologically astute sermons could directly relate to their lives. The application was up to the Holy Spirit.

Now I wonder how many times I hindered the Holy Spirit by giving nice theological talks without making sure it applied to the way in which people lived their lives. And if sermons don't apply to people's lives, how can people's lives be transformed?

Application Preaching for Life Change

If you were to write a purpose statement for preaching, what would it be? Let me suggest one purpose statement for preaching: *To help people become like Christ.*

That's what Paul writes in Romans 8:29, when he talks about people being called according to God's purpose: "For those whom he foreknew he also predestined *to be conformed to the image of his Son.*" Paul writes the same in 2 Corinthians 3:18: "And all of us . . . are being *transformed into the same image* from one degree of glory to another; for this comes from the Lord, the Spirit." And in Paul's great resurrection chapter he writes, "Just as we have borne the image of the man of dust, we will also bear *the image of the man of heaven*" (1 Corinthians 15:49).

In our *Lutheran Book of Worship (LBW)* liturgy we say these words: "Almighty God, you gave your Son both as a sacrifice for sin and a *model of the godly life.* Enable us to receive him always with thanksgiving, and to *conform our lives to his;* through the same Jesus Christ our Lord."[1] Besides being biblical, helping people become like Christ is also very Lutheran!

Rick Warren, in his "Application Preaching" workshops at Saddleback Church, stresses that helping people become like Christ means finding ways to help people think like Jesus, to feel like Jesus, and to act like Jesus.[2] This is much more than a simplistic WWJD (What Would Jesus Do?); it is a template for considering how to be most effective in preaching about the transforming power of a relationship with Jesus Christ. Let's think about those three ways to help people think, feel, and act like Jesus.

Thinking, Feeling, and Acting like Jesus

To help people think, feel, and act like Jesus, consider the preaching that touches the head, heart, and hands. This trilogy can also refer to the mind, will, and conduct or to convictions, character, and conduct.

They all have to do with thinking, feeling, and acting. And all three need to be engaged.

I was trained to be a "thinking" pastor. My goal was to preach logical, linear sermons. My Myers-Briggs Inventory is an ENTJ, with the "T" referring to Thinking. If something doesn't make sense to me, I don't do it. What speaks to me most are logical arguments and linear progression. When I first started preaching, I felt that everyone was the same as I am, and that there was a universal appreciation for linear thinking, head-oriented, mind-expanding, conviction-centered preaching.

I wish I knew then what I know now.

There is a relatively small percentage of people who value "thinking" and logical persuasion as much as I do. In the early days of my preaching, I thought I could argue people into God's kingdom because it was so logical. What I've learned is that some people's faith is driven by their hearts, while others are driven by expressing their faith with their hands—with "doing" through acts of service. I now realize that in my early preaching days I missed more than two-thirds of the people in the pew.

Thinking, feeling, and acting are expressions of faith that all need to be engaged in a sermon. To "think" like Jesus means that people's minds must be enlightened. The most common criticism from unchurched people about sermons is that they're boring, irrelevant, or just plain untrue about their life's experience. There's no excuse for the lack of solid exegetical work, since that's the major focus for pastors as they prepare each week.

For others, "feeling" is the way they connect to the sermon. Some people really engage when emotional stories are told from *Chicken Soup* or other resources. I am blessed that one of my associates preaches "feeling" sermons, since I'm not inclined that way. She reaches a portion of the congregation that I don't reach with my "thinking" kind of sermons. She helps us realize that being transformed by the power of a relationship with Jesus Christ means that people's hearts must be engaged so that people's character becomes more like Jesus.

A third way that reaches people in sermons is through "acting" like Jesus. This is not a simplistic emphasis on "works," but it stresses a message such as that found in Colossians 3:17, which tells us that everything we do, in word or deed, should be done in the name of Jesus. Notice the mention of the word *deed*. We should do whatever we do, in word or *deed*, in the name of Jesus. Sermons can be specific about equipping people's hands to "do" faith and to challenge them to consider how their conduct can become more like Jesus.

In this way there are three preaching mandates:

- ✹ Enlighten the mind, so that people can think like Jesus in their convictions (head).
- ✹ Engage the emotions, so that people can feel like Jesus in their character (heart).
- ✹ Challenge the will, so that people can act (hands) like Jesus in their conduct (hands).[3]

Application preaching begins with the trilogy of enlightening the mind, engaging the emotions, and challenging the will. Focusing on any one without the others falls short of the transforming power of knowing Jesus Christ.

The implication of this is that sermons should not be "information transfers" from the pastor to the people but be oriented toward life transformation. If the role of the pastor is to build up the body of Christ to full maturity and stature (Ephesians 4:11-13), then we need to focus on a variety of ways in which people can grow toward that full maturity.

Let me suggest three shifts that can be made in preaching.

Shift #1: From Lectionary to Series Preaching

Up until about five years ago I was a committed lectionary preacher.

I enjoyed the discipline that came from a flow of the church year that was complete with texts read on the same Sunday with many other churches across the country. I used to welcome people to worship with these words: "Welcome to church this morning on the twenty-third Sunday after Pentecost!"

What I found was that there were a dwindling number of people every year who were totally passionate about whether it was the thirteenth or the twenty-third Sunday after Pentecost. Instead, more and more people were wondering, "What does church mean for me in my life? How can I use biblical principles to learn how God wants me to live? How can being assured of my salvation help me make it through the dark times in my life? And does God have a purpose for my life?"

These are questions people struggle with and issues they want to think about, pray about, and hear about during Sunday morning worship. A sermon series can help focus on the exploration of those basic human needs.

A sermon series also enables the preacher and people to move from one place to the next. There's a flow and intentionality in preaching in a series. People often want to know where the preaching is going, and they are more likely to invite a friend if they know what the pastor will be preaching about.

To be sure, preaching a sermon series is very possible to do with the lectionary. Most pastors already preach sermon series during Advent and Lent. The Sundays after Easter present a very easy set of texts with which to preach a series on "The Truth about Faith" that can include issues of doubt, disobedience, and transformation. A sermon series on Revelation, Colossians, or First Corinthians can easily be constructed by using the lectionary. The point is not necessarily to abandon the lectionary; it's to organize preaching in such a way to capture a sense of momentum and anticipation.

In our congregation I spend several weeks in June every year setting up the sermon series for the next year from September through

June (July and August come later). I choose series outlines, lessons, sermon titles, and a three-sentence description of the "content target" for each sermon for each Sunday during the year. I often use the same texts that are used in the Revised Common Lectionary, but they're arranged in a different way through the series. In that way, all the notes, books, and resources that pastors have compiled over the years can be cross-referenced for use. You can see some sermon series examples at www.leadingonpurpose.org.

We begin each September with a sermon series on biblical leadership, since there are a lot of new people in leadership as the program year begins. It might be a series on The Leadership Vision of Jesus or Leadership Lessons from Nehemiah. Sunday school teachers, ministry teams, and those new to the congregation can learn about the leadership expectations of the congregation as each year begins.

In October/November we return to the lectionary for Reformation, All Saints, several Stewardship Sundays, and Christ the King. Advent and Christmas already have the best lectionary texts, so we keep those during those seasons.

During January/February we usually have a series on families, since Christmas is sometimes a difficult time for many families who deal with divorce or family strife or who remember the death of a loved one during the holidays. Healthy Habits of Faithful Families, Boundaries and Family Life, and Family Love Languages have served as sermon series during the past several years. This series theme also provides a good invitation to the many people who visit on Christmas Eve who are a part of the community. We invite them back by announcing a new series on Christmas Eve. What visitor doesn't want to come back and learn what the Bible says about building healthy families?

Lent is, of course, a time for an emphasis on spiritual maturity, and the lectionary texts often provide a series that are easily organized with a flow from one week to the next. Other series on spiritual maturity are equally appropriate.

The Sundays after Easter are also a good time to begin another series to "hook" the Easter visitors to bring them back for the next weeks. Again, the emphasis is to try to create anticipation and a flow from week to week, whether you use the lectionary or not. This is an especially good way to *enlighten the mind* for people who like sequential series that build each week.

Shift #2: From Information to Transformation

It was in my first parish, a wonderful, small, rural Wisconsin congregation that I tried my best to preach Bible-based lectionary sermons and, at the same time, keep up with all the "Special Emphasis" Sundays that were adopted at synod assemblies and suggested by the old ALC (American Lutheran Church). One such Special Emphasis Sunday in 1982 was "Ground Zero: Nuclear Awareness" Sunday. Being a dutiful pastor, I used the suggested texts, songs, litanies, and prayers that were included in the pastor's packet. I read the anti-war texts and preached against war and nuclear proliferation. I spoke eloquently about peace and justice and walking humbly with God. I felt a little strange about it, but that's what I felt I was supposed to do.

Right in the middle of the "Ground Zero" sermon, Stewart and his wife, who always sat in the third pew, stood up, put on their coats, and walked out. It destroyed my concentration, and people really didn't pay a lot of attention after that as they whispered to one another about why Stewart and his wife walked out.

That afternoon I called Stewart, just to see what was going on. "Stewart," I said, "I noticed that you left before the sermon was finished, and I figure you must have not felt good, or needed to go to a doctor's appointment, but I just wanted to call and check in about how things are going."

It probably would have been better not to have made that call.

For the next thirty minutes Stewart went on to blame me and "my types" for all the ills of the world, including ozone depletion, rainforest clear cutting, cultural moral decay, teenage pregnancy, the song "Alice's Restaurant," and radical feminism. He ended with these words that still ring in my ears: "I don't come to church to hear some young buck blow-hard spout off his mouth about things he don't know nothin' about."

I had used the pulpit for a social agenda information speech rather than a platform to witness to the life transforming power of a relationship with Jesus Christ. People don't need the kind of information that pastors are neither prepared nor qualified to preach about. What they need to know is the transforming power of knowing Jesus.

One of the best ways to do this is through personal testimonies that can be carefully prepared and coordinated between the pastor and the one giving the testimony. This isn't always an easy exercise for Lutherans! We're more accustomed to skits, stories, or movie clips during worship. All those are fine, but a testimony about transformation is singularly the best way to get a point across in a sermon. People watch skits and movie excerpts, and they listen to stories. But they're engaged with testimonies about a transformed life.

Testimonies generally have three parts: what one's life was before a transforming experience with Jesus, what caused the change, and what life has been like since that transformation. It's pretty simple and short, but it's very effective.

In preaching a three-point sermon on an aspect of prayer, for instance, a pastor can use a testimony to make the third point in a much more effective way than the pastor can by him or herself. The person giving the testimony needs to be carefully chosen, needs to be spiritually mature, and needs to be someone whom the pastor fully trusts. Again, this requires planning in advance—in some cases, several weeks in advance. It's most helpful to share the beginning part of the sermon with the person giving the testimony so it flows smoothly. People giving testimonies are honored that the pastor thought enough of them to invite them to become a partner in the delivery of the sermon. It's a great way to model ministry partnerships and shows a trust and respect for people as the pulpit is shared.

Another time for such a testimony is right before the offering is received. At our traditional service we say the offering prayer after the offering is received: "Merciful Father, we offer with joy and thanksgiving. . . ." At our other services we pray for people's hearts to be opened to God's will and way *before* the offering is received. Many Sundays we have a Ministry Moment that highlights one of the ministries of the congregation. This leads nicely into an offering prayer, especially if the Ministry Moment includes a personal testimony.

Any of these are good ways to *engage the emotions* for people who appreciate sermons and testimonies from the heart.

Shift #3: From Presentation to Asking for a Response or Commitment

Lutherans are often wary of things that sound like works righteousness. We generally don't like the letter of James, which says that faith without works is dead. We don't do altar calls, and we like to preach the gospel rather than make demands that seem like the law. Our emphasis is much more on *what God has done for us* rather than on *what we do for God*.

And yet people should be given the opportunity to respond to the sermon at least several times each month. It's like fishing. If you never reel in the line or haul in the net, you get no results. Many Lutheran sermons are like that.

The point in asking for a commitment in a sermon is not that God is going to love you more; rather a commitment means that you're going to love God more, and that's going to make all the difference in the world. This is especially a good way to *challenge the will* of those who need some way to respond to a sermon.

Let's think about this. In a recent four-part sermon series entitled The Direction of Our Church, the sermon titles revolved around our church being a place where the Spirit moves in, the pastor moves over, the people move up, and the church moves out. Any pastor could easily preach a four-part series just based on those titles.

The first week we asked for a commitment from people at the end of the sermon. With our response cards in every bulletin, we asked people to use the next four weeks to walk more closely with Jesus in their lives. What would be the signs of a Spirit moving in a congregation? That people were walking more closely with Christ? Wouldn't some signs be people reading their Bible more regularly; coming to church more often; giving more sacrificially of their time, talents, and treasures; and being more Christlike in the way they lived their lives? We asked people to write ICCW on their response cards (I Commit to a Closer Walk) if they agreed to these four commitments over the next four weeks. If they wrote their names on the response cards with ICCW, we told them that every day, for the next four weeks, the pastors would pray for them every morning by name. At the end of the sermon the pastor prayed for those willing to make such a commitment.

We received a response of about 60 percent of those in worship that day. A list was compiled by a volunteer, and the pastors prayed for the entire list by name every day for four weeks. Attendance during that time increased, giving increased, and the best outcome was being able to shake hands with people following the services and saying, "How's it going? I'm praying for your walk with Jesus every day." That's not law; it's gospel.

On the fourth Sunday, when we preached that our church is a place where the people move out, we asked people to personally commit to taking what they learned into their families, neighborhoods, and places of work. If we are truly a church of the Great Commission, we are to go to all nations and places where people don't believe and invite them into a life-transforming relationship with Jesus Christ. Again, we used the response cards to ask people to put a check by their names if they would commit to sharing the gospel with someone somewhere sometime in the next four weeks. That's not law; it's gospel.

Robert Fritch, senior pastor of Our Saviour Lutheran Church in Jamaica, Queens, New York City, serves a very traditional congregation. Recently he said, "Perhaps the greatest impact of the Purpose-Driven model has been on the application of my preaching."

> This year, during Lent, we made certain that people had something to put in their "faith toolbox." Every week we had a handout or postcard with simple tools that people could use on their faith journey during Lent. An example was what we did on Ash Wednesday. The sermon title was on "NOT Giving up Something for Lent," and it contained a list of things someone could "do" during Lent. Two of the more than twenty examples on Ash Wednesday were these: Fast from hostility and feast on tenderness; fast from bitterness and feast on forgiveness. We had about 250 people in church on Ash Wednesday, but we gave out over 600 cards. People were taking them for family, friends, and co-workers; in fact we printed up more for the following Sunday. The next Sunday, two previously uninvolved people came up to me after worship and said they had been thinking about my sermon and they wanted to "do" something. One is now organizing a joint youth group event with another church that has no youth leaders, and the other is in the approval phase of beginning a prison outreach ministry to Riker's Island.

That's not law; it's gospel. Robert concluded by saying, "People are hungry, but we're feeding them nothing but sugar. What they really want is something that will make them more fulfilled."

There's no more important place for you to learn how to share the gospel than in your local congregation. And the most important time to learn how to share that is in the sermon on Sunday morning. Pastors have an incredible opportunity to share the transforming experience of knowing Christ, and they need the support and encouragement of church leaders in order to do so. With this partnership, there can be a congregational focus on *enlightening the mind, engaging the emotions,* and *challenging the will* of all those who come to worship with you.

In the next chapter we'll explore the purpose to which this is directed.

Questions for Discussion

1. What is your response to thinking, feeling, and acting like Jesus? Is it too simplistic? Why or why not? If you are a pastor, what do you expect from people after they listen to a sermon? If you are a "listener," what do you expect from a sermon?

2. What do you think about the idea in this chapter that encouraging people to "do" something is the gospel, and not "law" oriented? How can you proclaim the gospel in your congregation?

3. How does flexibility in lectionary preaching work? What can you do to support your pastor in preaching sermon series, with or without the lectionary?

4. What do you think about asking for a commitment in the sermon? How would that be received in your congregation?

6

A Lutheran Reading of The Purpose-Driven Life

Imagine. Just imagine.

Imagine the impact on your congregation and in your community if the members of your congregation were committed to discovering and living out God's purpose for their lives. Imagine what your congregation and your community would look like if people were seriously committed to discipleship and Bible study, to coming regularly to worship, to being in a small group, to sharing their faith with others, and to discovering ways in which they can serve God in their daily lives. Isn't that what you wish for every member of your congregation?

For some it remains a dream. For others it has become a reality. Rick Warren has taken the work he has done with *The Purpose-Driven Church* and developed it into a personal faith journey in *The Purpose-Driven Life: What on Earth Am I Here For?*[1]

Taking the five purposes of the church—worship, evangelism, discipleship, fellowship, and ministry—Warren has suggested that these purposes are not just purposes of the church, but the purposes for the life of every Christian. Fully devoted followers of Jesus Christ should realize that they were planned for God's pleasure (worship), made for a mission (evangelism), created to become like Christ (discipleship), formed for God's family (fellowship), and shaped for serving God (ministry). In order to capture these purposes for the individual life of a Christian, Warren has written *The Purpose-Driven Life*.

The Purpose-Driven Life: The Book

Rick Warren has hit a nerve with his book *The Purpose-Driven Life* with the captivating subtitle: *What on Earth Am I Here For?* It spent many weeks on the *New York Times* best-seller list, is prominently displayed at many bookstores, and has already sold 16 million copies.

The book begins with these words:

> This is more than a book; it is a guide to a 40-day spiritual journey that will enable you to discover the answer to life's most important question: What on earth am I here for? By the end of this journey you will know God's purpose for your life and will understand the big picture—how all the pieces of your life fit together. Having this perspective will reduce your stress, simplify your decisions, increase your satisfaction, and, most important, prepare you for eternity.[2]

Those are some pretty big claims!

Warren begins by discussing the question of the purpose of one's life and correctly states that it all starts with God. Even to begin answering the question of one's existence, you must start with God, and not with you.

Having said that, Warren goes on through the Forty Days to underscore that the five purposes of the church found in the Great Commission and the Great Commandment are also purposes of people's lives. Each one of us needs to have a balance in our lives of worship, evangelism, fellowship, discipleship, and ministry to lead a balanced Christian life. These are explored in captivating chapters that are easy to read and understand.

Warren seeks to answer the question "Why am I here?" by offering a balance with these purposes:

- You were planned for God's pleasure (Worship)
- You were formed for God's family (Fellowship)

- You were created to become like Christ (Discipleship)
- You were shaped for serving God (Ministry)
- You were made for a mission (Evangelism)

This easy outline makes this a captivating book and is part of the reason for its success. Pastors and leaders will want to be very familiar with the book if it is being discussed within the congregation.

There are some clear Lutheran objections to Warren's book. Some have correctly written that Warren does not have a proper knowledge of the use of the Means of Grace (Baptism and the Lord's Supper) and that he lacks an understanding of total human sinfulness. Others are bothered by the lack of differentiation between law and gospel and a misunderstanding of the difference between justification and sanctification. His use of Scripture is often quite random; he quotes one thousand Bible verses from a variety of translations that are often chosen because of the use of a particular word that supports the specific point he's trying to make.

Let me just highlight one major difference between Warren's theology and Lutheran theology that may be instructive. It revolves around the question, "Who is driving the verbs?" That is, who is the subject of the sentence? In Warren's theology people are saved in order to give honor to God. For Lutherans, we are saved and loved by God because of what Christ has done for us. Some Lutherans believe that Warren has written a book that borders on semi-Pelagianism, which teaches that we have the capacity to seek God by our own will and our own works without any movement or involvement on God's part. Put more simply, some Lutherans believe that Warren's book stresses what we do for God more than what we receive from God.

Nonetheless, with that in mind, if pastors, church councils, and congregational members read *The Purpose-Driven Life* alongside Luther's Small Catechism, some exciting things can begin to happen. People begin to identify more clearly what it means to be

Lutheran and how *The Purpose-Driven Life* can help deepen their understanding of God's will and way for their lives. Warren's book has helped thousands of Lutherans become more fully devoted followers of Jesus Christ and has deepened their understanding of what it means to be Lutheran.

One helpful resource for working with this material is an "Up for Discussion" guide on *The Purpose-Driven Life* available at www.augsburgfortress.org. It's a reproducible discussion guide to be used with groups, and it can serve as an introduction or overview of the book. God, Baptism, worship, and purpose are four major themes explored in this resource. It summarizes what Warren says about each one, then looks at each through a Lutheran Lens, and explores a Digging In paragraph, in which participants are asked to think more deeply about a Lutheran understanding of these topics. Other helpful web resources for Lutherans have been compiled by Pastor Robert Driver-Bishop at www.purposedrivenlutherans.com.

The Purpose-Driven Life: The Campaign

Warren's book has been the centerpiece of a 40 Days of Purpose Campaign that was used in 20,000 churches in 2004. Far from being a "blip on the map" or a fad, this campaign and its follow-ups are going to be around for a number of years.

The campaign utilizes resources for weekend worship, sermons, and music, along with a Simulcast, small group video discussion guides, bookmarks, and a vast variety of resources to tailor the campaign to your congregation. Rather than describe them here, it's best to spend time at www.purposedriven.com. There you'll see how the campaign is based on unified prayer, concentrated focus, multiple reinforcements, behavioral teaching, and exponential thinking.

At St. Matthew we used the 40 Days of Purpose Campaign during Lent of 2003, and it was very well received by the congregation. We preached about the five purposes for the life of a

Christian during each of the five Sundays, had small groups, and encouraged people to buy and read the book. I communicated with about 150 people with a daily e-mail devotional guide that I wrote on each of the chapters of the book. Those e-mails are available at www.leadingonpurpose.org.

The cost to buy in to the campaign depends on the worship size of the congregation. The amount of material that is given is a little overwhelming, but it's very well done, and there is a multitude of support material available to order or to view online.

We weren't able to do every aspect of the Campaign, simply because it was Lent. It's best to conduct the Campaign when your full efforts can be devoted to it and when you can get a team of people working together to make the Campaign as successful as it can be.

The Purpose-Driven Life: The Results

"This has been an amazing experience, to say the least," said Jay Hilbinger of First Lutheran Church in Greensboro, North Carolina.

> We have never had any more than 150 to 200 adults engaged in any kind of discipleship groups, classes, or spiritual growth at any given time. On a weekly basis, during the program year, we used to have about 125 to 150 adults involved, which includes Sunday classes and other weekday, weeknight groups and classes. We also had about a dozen or fewer small groups that only met once a month, and most of them are more about fellowship than any intentional spiritual growth. We had another half dozen or so monthly dinner groups. We have about 1,550 baptized members on the books, and worship around 500 to 600 a Sunday during three morning services and one evening service. There are about 700 households in our 1,550 membership.

As we began the 40 Days of Purpose Campaign, we suddenly had more than 500 people involved in small groups and class, as well as home groups. We distributed around 800 Purpose-Driven Life books. On our kickoff weekend we had 755 in worship, even though our evening service snowed out! The next weekend we had 949 in worship. We've trained and are using 42 facilitators, about half of whom have never led any adult groups or classes before this. The most we have ever had in combined worship (other than Christmas Eve and Easter), prior to last Sunday, was 907 on the Sunday after 9-11-2001.

"It's a cliché," Jay said, "but if God builds it, they will come."

Harlen Menk, pastor at English Lutheran in the small town of Ellsworth, Wisconsin, said something similar.

We started in May and took five months getting ready and jumping through all the hoops according to the plan. We launched the campaign in October. I called it the "full-meal-deal" approach. The results were incredible. We pulled out all the stops, spent lots of money, and got an incredible lesson in how to do evangelism. We formed 37 small groups with nearly 300 people in attendance. That's a number equal to our weekly worship attendance! Nine groups remain where there were none before, and we expect to see those numbers grow. Worship attendance went up 35 percent during the campaign and continues to be strong. I have a long list of people waiting to be a part of our next membership class.

I asked Harlen whether First English sacrificed their solid Lutheran theology. "Perish the thought," Harlen said. "We're still good Lutherans here. And we still celebrate Holy Communion every Sunday at every service. We still teach Luther's *Small Catechism* just like we always have. But these principles have been the best thing to happen to my ministry since I left seminary twenty-six years ago."

At Saddleback Church, where Rick Warren is the senior pastor, 14,000 people gather for worship each weekend. When they did their first 40 Days of Purpose Campaign in the fall of 2002, they received 671 new believers and 1,200 new members. Their worship attendance increased by 2,000 each weekend, and they started 2,400 new home Bible study groups.

The first 8,000 congregations who participated in the 40 Days of Purpose Campaign averaged 20 percent growth in worship attendance and a 102 percent average increase in small group participation.

But it's not about numbers, and it's certainly not about success. It's about life transformation through a relationship with Jesus Christ. One eighth grade girl in a Lutheran congregation that had just begun the 40 Days Campaign picked up her mother's book and started reading the first several chapters. The next Wednesday evening at confirmation, she told her pastor, "I really like the book; it's been helpful. I have a friend at school who has been talking about committing suicide because he likes this girl and she doesn't like him. Anyway, I told him that he wasn't an accident. I mean his life isn't an accident. God has a purpose—a lot of them—for his life."

She is in eighth grade. And she may have saved a life.

That's what this is all about. It's about realizing that God created us to be one-of-a-kind people, with a purpose for our lives. We are neither accidents nor the evolutionary by-products of multiple, random genetic mutations. One of the most important aspects of leading on purpose is to be able to cast a vision of what this means for people's lives to be fully devoted followers of Jesus Christ. There isn't anything more important that can happen in someone's life than to discover and then live out the purpose for which God has created them.

The Purpose-Driven Life: The Follow-up

During the 40 Days of Purpose Campaign people are asked repeatedly to examine the meaning, direction, vision, and purpose of their lives. People are given biblical examples of lives lived on purpose, and most congregations hear very captivating testimonies from people during the campaign. People hear about living on three levels: the level of survival, the level of success, and the level of significance.

The level of *survival* means just doing what you need to do to get by. It's getting up in the morning and instead of saying, "Good Morning, Lord!" saying "Good Lord, it's morning."

The level of *success* is the level of working hard at succeeding at work, at home, or at school, with the constant fear of failure and the nagging fear that no amount of any kind of success will be enough.

But the level of *significance* comes with knowing that you're doing exactly what God put you on this earth to do, and you're making a significant contribution with your life to your ministry within the church and your mission in the world. The level of significance means that you're comfortable with is your Tombstone Testimony, which we'll talk about in the final chapter. The 40 Days Campaign helps people move toward discovering that kind of significance in their lives. But what happens when the campaign ends?

At that point, it's best not to go back to the "twenty-third Sunday after Pentecost."

At St. Matthew we took a longer view of the 40 Days Campaign: we stretched out our emphasis to include a summer sermon series, Dare to Dream! We described that series in this way:

> What did you want to be when you grew up?
>
> Many of us had dreams of being astronauts or movie stars or doctors or baseball players. What happened to those dreams? Some of us continued dreaming, even though our dreams

changed. But others were scarred by the disappointment of those lost goals, or we grew comfortable and complacent, and we stopped dreaming.

God also has dreams, or plans, for us, but many Christians have stopped dreaming, or even wanting to get closer to the dream that God might have for us. In this summer sermon series you'll be invited to dream again. It will take some courage. Dreams open you up to disappointment, perhaps even ridicule, but they can also bring great joy and satisfaction. Worship with us and dare to dream.

In the summer series we looked carefully at the dreams that God put in the hearts of Joseph, Gideon, David, Judas, Hannah, Peter, Jonah, Mary, and Jesus. We talked about discovery, dreams, life transformation, and living for significance rather than success. Over the course of the summer we included several testimonies about that discovery process. We sang songs and hymns that had to do with being used for God's purpose. We ended sermons with commitment and discovery prayers.

During the summer series I also put a lot of time into preparing an e-mail series that I sent out to about 150 people three times a week. I called it the "Dare to Dream Personal Commitment." It was an e-mail journey that supplemented the sermon series. I told people that I was doing this because I passionately believe that God has created each and every one of us for significance. That significance might not be to change the world; it might be to be an incredible husband or friend or teacher or business leader. But I believe that God has much more than mediocrity in mind for each and every one of us. Jesus gave totally of himself because that's what God wanted of him, and we're called to do the same of ourselves for the sake of others.

Each Friday I sent an e-mail about the coming Sunday's theme and included the sermon text and the weekly devotional that people

have written. I also included my own textual comments that were done in preparation but that I didn't have the chance to weave into the sermon. On Monday I sent exercises to help people think through the theme and how it relates to their lives. Personal dream exercises were a part of these Monday e-mails. Then on Wednesday we went on a "God Hunt" and talked about seeing how God is present in our lives every day. All this is available for review at www.leadingonpurpose .org, along with other resources and sermon audios.

We started the Dare to Dream! series on Pentecost Sunday and gave an overview of what the series was going to be about. We asked people to check the response box on our response cards if they were willing to make a Pentecost Pledge, which included the following commitments:

- Attend worship more regularly this summer than last summer.
- Commit to saying something positive about St. Matthew to at least one person each month this summer who is not part of a worshiping community.
- Keep your offering current even if you are out of town.

Again, we told people that if they signed the Pentecost Pledge, the pastors would pray for them by name at least once each week during the summer months. More than three hundred people signed the Pentecost Pledge. We didn't experience the typical summer slump in worship attendance or giving, and we had a great group of new members join the next fall.

Most important, we experienced a growth in the number of people involved in ministry teams or starting new ministry teams. People dared to dream about what God might want to do with their lives, and they started living into those dreams. Our people don't experience being asked to make these kinds of commitments as law, because they know the gospel experience of committing themselves to something significant.

If you are going to step into the 40 Days of Purpose Campaign, be sure to plan for what you're going to do once people discover

God's purpose for their lives! Most likely you won't achieve the "numbers success" that some other churches have experienced. But you will discover that people will be asking more significant questions about their lives than they ever have before. And if you haven't prepared an infrastructure, or a plan for what to do with those questions and the responses that it elicits, you'll probably fall short of the impact that you might have otherwise had.

By now you're probably catching on to what it means to be leading on purpose, and you probably already have a plan for what you'd like to do in your congregation. Let's talk next about how to make some of the necessary transitions to leading on purpose. It's a long-term process that requires a lot of planning and prayer!

Questions for Discussion

1. What do you find to be true in this chapter? Where do you find disagreement? Do you agree or disagree with Warren's idea that fully devoted followers of Jesus should have a personal balance on worship, evangelism, fellowship, discipleship, and ministry?

2. How would you describe the theological differences that are talked about in this chapter? What can we learn from someone who has a different theological perspective?

3. What is your life's purpose? What do you think that God has created you for and called you to do? Are you on your way to fulfilling that purpose?

4. What is your congregation doing to cast a vision of what it means for people to be fully devoted followers of Jesus Christ? What paths or steps are clearly identified, or are they more random? What changes can be made to make the process more clearly defined?

7

Transitioning to Leading on Purpose

Almost all congregations have experienced conflict, are experiencing conflict, or will experience conflict in the next short while. Ambivalence in mainline churches is reaching epidemic proportions. Suggesting change that might rock the fragile core of many congregations is something that many pastors and church councils fear doing. Transitioning to truly leading on purpose can bring you directly into the midst of conflict, because it suggests a different way of doing things. For a traditional church that is used to "doing church" in the way they've always done things, change can be very difficult.

Remember that conflict is inevitable. Combat isn't.

In order to introduce some of the changes that we've been talking about in this book you'll have to use "systems thinking." That means that what is happening in one "system" of your congregation will affect all the other parts of the church. Leading on purpose is not just a program or a simple strategy. It is changing the spiritual DNA of your congregation.

Peter Steinke has done masterful work with *Healthy Congregations: A Systems Approach*.[1] In his book, tapes, and talks on the subject he discusses three parts, or priorities, of the human brain.

The lower brain is the reptilian, reactive, defensive part of the brain that was designed to protect us. When we are attacked or threatened we react from this part of the brain. One of the attributes of this part of the brain is that it has no concept of time. Things that scared us as children often scare us as adults. I distinctly remember being in third grade, walking down the street, and hearing a noise behind me. I turned around and was face to face with a large German shepherd that barked, bared his teeth, and splattered dog slobber on my face. The hair on my neck stood on end, my heart pounded, and I was terrified of being eaten alive. My reaction came from the reptilian, reactive part of my brain, and to this day, when I am surprised by a barking dog, I immediately revert to those same feelings.

The second part of the brain is the mammalian, relational part of the brain, where play, bonding, and feelings are located. This part of the brain still doesn't deal with things on a totally rational plane but is limbic and playful.

The third part of the brain is the neocortex, where we do our thinking, imagining, visioning, and reflecting. When we get to dealing with issues in our neocortex, we can deal with issues with clarity and objectivity. When we are facing change and conflict and anxiety, however, we often become driven by the reactive part of the brain. We want to defend ourselves against what we perceive as threats to our safety or stability. When anxiety is high, the reaction to that anxiety is drawn from the lower part of the brain.

The same happens in congregational life. When a pastor or church leader suggests changes in preaching, worship, organizational structure, committees, new member process, or wants to ask congregational members to make a discipleship commitment, the change can produce anxiety, because "it's never been done that way before." Changes in stable, traditional congregations can lead to conflict, which most pastors and leaders want to avoid. The higher the anxiety, the lower the reaction. This is why changes that result in increased anxiety bring up all kinds of old memories of someone who did something to someone twenty years ago. The reactive part of the brain has no sense of time having passed, and so those memories rage to the surface as if they just happened. And the pastor and church leaders are left wondering what happened.

When change happens, it produces anxiety. And what many anxious situations need most is exactly what they can't get, that is, our Christian values that come from thinking and processing change in our neocortex. If we operate with the lower parts of our brains, we sometimes neglect our Christian values. But when change is introduced in calm, rational, nondefensive ways, then constructive Christian conversation can happen with neocortex values.

In his book *Transitioning,* Dan Southerland writes these words:

> Anyone who is trying to do something for God will face some opposition. There is always opposition when you lead the church through transition. There will be opposition from those who do not understand the change. There will be opposition from those who understand the change but just don't like it. There will be opposition from those whose kingdom you are messing with. There will be opposition from those people whom the enemy controls. There will be opposition from those people who just love to be contrary. You have each of these groups in your church.[2]

Changing your congregation's mode of operating takes much longer than most people think. I often tell people that good change usually takes twice as long as your most pessimistic projections, but when it happens, it is twice as good as your most optimistic dreams because it's good, deep, systemic change.

One Congregation's Story of Change

Bethlehem Lutheran Church in south Minneapolis is a large, urban congregation with a 110-year history. It is a congregation that was served well by its pastors, reaching a membership of more than 3,000 members in the 1960s when young families filled the area. Slowly, over time, the congregational membership plateaued and began a slow decline that lasted several decades, as more and more families moved out to the suburbs.

In 1997 a group of leaders and staff from Bethlehem Lutheran went to Saddleback Church in southern California for a Purpose-Driven Church conference. With the synergy that developed at the conference, each of the church leaders and staff became convinced that this was a model that would transform and inspire the life of the congregation. Greg Meyer, executive pastor at Bethlehem, was so convinced that this was the model for the congregation that he completely rewrote his Sunday sermon on the flight back home on Saturday, and he has never preached the same way since.

At one of the next church council meetings, the pastors (Greg Meyer, Chris Nelson, and Tania Haber) wrote the Great Commission and the Great Commandment in big letters on poster board. They took some time at the church council meeting and asked, "What do these two statements from Jesus tell us that the church should be about?" In a fairly short time, the church council identified the purposes of worship, evangelism, fellowship, discipleship, and ministry. Some words were a little different, but the purposes were the same.

At another church council meeting they constructed a new membership covenant,[3] which included a commitment to protect the unity of the church, share the responsibility of the church, serve in the ministry of the church, and support the testimony of the church. They asked the church council to also commit to this covenant, and the transformation process began in earnest.

They developed a discipleship process that took into account the concentric circles of commitment and the STAR of Bethlehem. Instead of using the model of the baseball diamond, Bethlehem used the process of Starting (new member class), Transforming (spiritual maturity), Affirming (gift discovery), and Reaching (ministry). After the Starting classes for new members had been in session for a while, there began a "buzz" from some of the older, more traditional members wanting to know what was being taught to the new members, who came in with a high level of commitment and participation. Over the next several years about 400 long-term members went through the Starting class. They became revitalized in their walk of faith by knowing what was being expected from the new members through the class and through the membership covenant.

Eventually the leadership of Bethlehem began to focus on their target audience. In a city full of Lutherans, they began to ask, "Why would someone come to church here if they weren't in the habit of doing so?" They decided that the targets they could most easily reach were people with a good church memory who value good church music and traditional worship. They found that they could best reach people who listened to Minnesota Public Radio in their cars.

They then began to completely restructure their Sunday educational forums to become faith formation classes with a focus. The number of people engaged in learning opportunities have grown more than fourfold in the past eight years. Worship attendance has grown from 700 to 1,250. Giving has doubled, going from $750,000 to $1,500,000. Giving to benevolence has greatly increased through two capital stewardship campaigns: last year Bethlehem gave away $300,000 and is one of the largest contributors to the ELCA in the synod. A new postmodern worship site (Spirit Garage) has started to reach people in the Uptown area who probably would never set foot in the Gothic style cathedral where Bethlehem worships. Bethlehem has hosted several Transition Conferences put on by Saddleback. Bethlehem's pastors teach workshops not only around the country but also at Saddleback. Tania Haber was the first female pastor to teach at Saddleback, and Chris Nelson has made several trips to teach Purpose-Driven classes in India. In 1999 Bethlehem won the "Church Health Award" at Saddleback.

It's a story of deep, systemic, transitional change that happened in an urban congregation that only has traditional *LBW* worship but does everything exceptionally well and isn't afraid to make mistakes. There are now more fully devoted followers of Jesus at Bethlehem than there have ever been, and there is great congregational spiritual vitality.

Specific Steps toward Transformational Change

The most helpful change process that many churches can use is a process modeled on John Kotter's book *Leading Change*.[4] His main thesis is that systemic change and successful transformation follow a specific pattern with steps that must be honored. If steps are taken out of sequence, the results of transformation are undermined. To fully understand the process it's important to read both Kotter's and Southerland's books. The basic steps of transformational change are summarized below, with an adaptation to congregational life.

1. Make personal preparation. Bringing transformational change to the life of a congregation is a long-term, difficult process. Pastors and leaders who are not willing to invest their time and energy and passion should not even begin the process. It requires courage, conviction, and stamina to transform the life of a congregation.

Before any transformation change is begun, it's instructive to read the story of Nehemiah. Nehemiah, the king's cupbearer, after hearing the story of the destruction of the walls of Jerusalem, first spent time mourning, fasting, and praying before God (Nehemiah 1:4). In all, he prayed and fasted for several months to discern the will of God for his life. He came to see that God's vision for him was to rebuild and transform the walls of Jerusalem. Southerland writes, "Vision is usually given to those who pray until they get it. If prayer is not the octane that fuels your vision, your vision will stall out and your church will be motionless."[5] Discernment of vision only comes for those who are willing to wait patiently for God's vision. Pastors and leaders who do not make personal preparation for transformation by immersing themselves in prayer for God's guidance will fail even before they begin.

There were several times in my past when I tried to initiate change in congregational life before I was personally prepared to lead the change. In those days I would pray this prayer: "Dear Lord, please bless what I'm doing." I was convinced that the change was a good change, it made sense, and all I needed was for God to agree with me!

In the past several years, after initiating long-term, systemic change at St. Matthew, I have become convinced of the need for this first step. Now my prayer is this: "Dear Lord, please let me do what you're blessing." God is in charge of the vision. It's my role to discern that vision; it's God's role to give it. Once God's vision is discerned, it can be defined much more clearly.

2. Create a sense of urgency for the discerned vision. Pastors and leaders must encourage a sense of "holy discontent" by pointing out the difference between what currently exists and where God is calling the congregation. Having done the personal preparation, leaders need to ask, "What will happen if we don't make this change?" If the answer is that nothing will happen, then there is no reason to make the change because there is no sense of urgency. Churches are often resistant to change because many people just don't see the benefit of going through the change process.

One way to do this is to point out the difference (the gap) between the current situation and what you discern the purpose of God is for your congregation. This sense of urgency must be conveyed with passion, but without blame or a sense of shame for those who have not caught the vision or those who have caught it but disagree! A careful balance must be kept. Too much urgency leads to a loss of hope, and not enough urgency breeds complacency.

When I started at St. Matthew in December 1997, the congregation had just been through a very difficult time. The beloved senior pastor and several key program and pastoral staff had left before some of the transitions they had envisioned had come to fruition. When I arrived, several key lay leaders encouraged me to become familiar with the Purpose-Driven Church materials and go to a workshop at Saddleback, from where they had just returned. I was not really impressed, but said I would if I could find the time.

Several staff members went to Saddleback shortly after I arrived and learned more about the Purpose-Driven Church model. They also came to me and said, "Eric, this model will really work well at St. Matthew. God has put all the pieces in place, and now is the time to move on this." Again, I said that I would if I could but that it just wasn't an urgent concern or calling of mine.

By the time I went with two staff people to Saddleback, I had been at St. Matthew for almost a year, and I became convinced that this was the model that God wanted us to use to transform the life of the congregation. I was captivated by a sense of urgency that this wasn't the product of "just another program" but was the means by which we could help develop fully devoted followers of Jesus Christ at St. Matthew. I began the personal preparation that resulted in a sense of urgency for God's vision.

We began by preaching a sermon series on The Purpose of St. Matthew and spent five weeks talking about the Great Commission and the Great Commandment. We preached about the important emphasis on worship, evangelism, fellowship, discipleship, and ministry. Later, we spent ten weeks reading through *The Purpose-Driven Church* with the staff (actually, we did it twice!), and we spent another five months using it for our Board devotions and discussion. Eventually, over time, the staff, Board, and other key leaders began to catch a sense of urgency for the kind of transformation that was truly needed at St. Matthew.

3. Establish a vision team. Once there has been personal preparation, a discernment of the vision, and a sense of urgency, it's time to establish a vision team. Follow the important steps in chapter 4 for establishing a team, and be sure to include a diverse group of leaders, managers, dreamers, and influencers who have a deep commitment to Christ and a high level of trust within the congregation.

A vision team is a group effort and needs to include people who are spiritually mature and supportive of transformational change. Above all, this vision team must be able to commit to praying together frequently, even in the midst of a meeting, and be able to discern what God is blessing.

The vision team at English Lutheran in Ellsworth, Wisconsin, met for two years putting together their mission statement of "Transforming Lives through Christ Centered Community" and identifying their target groups, which included:

- Geographically: All those living within thirty minutes driving time.
- Demographically: Households with children under eighteen living at home.
- Culturally: Those who invest their time in their children's school and sports activities and enjoy outdoor recreation; those who prefer beer to wine, enjoy "pop-rock" music, and eat burgers, brats, and pizza.
- Spiritually: People with a positive church memory.

By now they were ready to create a new structure in order to reach their target audience and bring those in the community into the crowd, congregation, and finally, the core.

4. Communicate the vision. There are multitudes of ways to construct the important link between the vision team and the congregation. If the congregation doesn't hear about the vision and if there isn't a sense of urgency, the chances are pretty likely that the vision will remain in the hearts of a few leaders but will never come to fruition within the congregation. As we talked about at the beginning of this chapter, change often produces anxiety, and the higher the anxiety, the more difficult it is to deal with change using Christian values, which are in the neocortex of the brain.

One way to link the vision team and the congregation is by asking questions that lead and inspire people to think about the vision for themselves. "What would it look like if we became a congregation that fully implemented the Great Commandment to love people around us? What would we need to change in order to reach out to all nations? What would the signs be of a congregation that was fully committed to the Great Commission?" In that way, people can begin the dreaming vision in their own minds, rather than being forced into a vision that is only owned by the pastor and leaders.

The vision for transformation needs to be clear, reasonable, and precise, and it should be implemented with metaphors, stories, and examples of life change. Forums, feedback, surveys, and other modes of communication can help broadcast the vision broadly and reach people in a variety of ways.

After all this has taken place, it's time for the pastor to do some deep reflection before the next step is taken. The pastor needs to ask, "Am I willing to make the personal adjustments to God's calling in order to lead this transformational process? Am I willing to make a commitment to the congregation of the years of time that are necessary to implement this vision? And am I convinced that I can do nothing other than respond to this vision?" Those who are willing to fully answer "yes" to all these questions are able to enter into the incredibly exciting and rewarding transformation process of leading on purpose.

5. Determine the path and implement the vision. Change needs to be implemented prayerfully, slowly, strategically, and carefully. Remember that transformation is a long-term process! It isn't for the faint of heart, and it isn't something that a pastor should lead unless he or she is willing to see the changes through in a congregation. Many pastors only stay in their calls for four to five years, and in that amount of time there is hardly the chance to determine whether or not transformational change can truly happen. The kind of change that is involved in this book is at least a six- to eight-year process.

The vision for leading on purpose needs to be implemented

strategically. At St. Matthew we used our new member class and membership covenant for two years before we preached a four-part series on what it means to be a member of St. Matthew. In that way we "grandfathered in" all the people who had joined in the previous 58-year history of the congregation. A year after that, when we had been teaching our Spiritual Maturity class for two years, we preached a five-part series on spiritual maturity and the habits of prayer, daily devotion, financial giving, and fellowship. A year after that, when we had been teaching our SHAPE class for two years, we preached a series about Spiritual Gifts, Heart, Abilities, Personality, and Experience and how each one of us is uniquely gifted for a ministry in the church and a mission in the world. A year after that we developed a guide for starting a ministry team that has turned out to be extremely valuable, even though we had been working with ministry teams for three years before we developed the guide!

In order to truly implement the vision and determine the path, it's important to put key leaders to work in places where they are most passionately gifted. When Nehemiah worked to rebuild the walls of Jerusalem, he put his initial efforts into rebuilding the gates because he knew that the gates were the most visible places where people could see the benefits of rebuilding the walls (see Nehemiah 3:1-15, 28). After the visible success of such a public victory of rebuilding, he engaged the people to work *where they were most passionate about working,* at the section closest to their homes (see Nehemiah 3:23-30). In order to build the best team for implementing the vision and determining the path, put people in leadership in areas they are most passionate about so that passion can be best utilized and focused.

This is a time-consuming process. It might even take several years to make personal preparation with the pastors, staff, and key leaders (year one), create a sense of urgency (year two), establish a vision team and begin to make small changes (year three), and begin to implement some of the major changes that will transform the spiritual DNA of your congregation (year four).

6. Create short-term "wins" to reinforce momentum. You know how your congregation celebrates best. Creating short-term wins is important in keeping the change process in front of the congregation. Celebrating progress is a way of recognizing leaders who have led some of the change, and testimonies can be very helpful in creating a sense of reinforcement for the vision. "Thermometer" charts are fairly unimaginative, so think of creative ways in which you can publicly recognize when a short-term win is achieved.

Commission a ministry team. Show pictures of new children in Sunday school. Have an interview during the sermon with someone who recently became a Christian. Tell stories of adult baptisms. Bless a new carpet. Lay hands on the vision team. Develop a compelling slogan. You know how to do this best in your congregation, but remember that the transformational process is not complete until the entire congregation is aligned with the vision. Short-term wins reinforce the momentum in the same way that a pinch of yeast leavens the whole loaf.

Finally, remember to keep the sense of urgency in front of the congregation. The transformational vision that we've been talking about through this book will determine new priorities for the congregation and will launch new initiatives for years to come.

Leading on purpose is a personal journey that has deeply transformational implications. Robert Quinn, in his book *Deep Change*, writes, "Organization and change are not complementary concepts."[6] If momentum dies, the vision for change begins to die, and the congregation begins a slow process of going back to "the way things were." Deep change means a change in the spiritual DNA of your congregation, and it begins with a deep, personal change in the hearts of the pastor and church leaders. Quinn writes:

There is an important link between deep change at the personal level and deep change at the organizational level. To make deep personal change is to develop a new paradigm, a new self, one that is more effectively aligned with today's realities. . . . In doing so, we learn the paradoxical lesson that we can change the world only by changing ourselves.[7]

Questions for Discussion

1. What have been some of the major changes that have happened in your congregation in the last five years? What was the level of anxiety? If there was anxiety, what caused it? If there wasn't, what helped the change go smoothly?

2. What do you expect from your members? Do you consider your congregation to be a high- or low-commitment congregation? What things could you do to raise the level of commitment?

3. What do you think about the six steps toward transformation? Where are you now? What are the next steps you need to take?

4. What can you do to keep a sense of urgency in front of the congregation so that the vision stays alive and fresh?

8

Leading on Purpose:
Visioning a Faithful Future
for Those You Serve

I am the LORD your God . . . showing steadfast love to the thousandth generation of those who love me and keep my commandments. (Exodus 20:2, 6)

The thousandth generation is a really long time. It's at least 2,400 years, which stretches from our time back until long before Jesus was even born. Those are the long-term effects of a relationship with God that is lived in faith, love, commitment, and life transformation. That's the vision God has for those who love God.

In Genesis 12, when God's call got personal with Abram, God said, "Go from your country and your kindred and your father's house. . . . And I will make of you a great nation." In other places where God reiterated this promise, God told Abram that his offspring would be like the dust of the earth that cannot be counted (Genesis 13:16), and as many as the stars of the heavens and the sand on the seashore (Genesis 22:17). The promise began when God said "Go" and Abram went. God was calling Abram to be a fully devoted follower. That's the vision God had for Abram.

When Isaac spoke a blessing to Jacob he said these words in Genesis 27:28-29:

May God give you of the dew of heaven, and of the fatness of the earth, and plenty of grain and wine. Let peoples serve you, and nations bow down to you . . . and blessed be everyone who blesses you!

This vision of a special future was Jacob's destiny. Isaac blessed Jacob, giving him something to look forward to for the rest of his life.

Is there a way in which pastors and leaders can give the people they serve some kind of vision for a life close with God that has implications for generations to come? When pastors and leaders lead on purpose, is there a place for the articulation of a captivating vision that will give people something to look forward to for the rest of their lives?

In this final chapter I'd like to ask you for a commitment similar to the commitment that I ask from people as I end many of my sermons. Read through the following four questions, which are followed by additional explanation. At the end of each of the sections, circle the number that reflects how strongly you feel about your answer to the question. Don't share it with anyone. Just reflect on your personal commitment to leadership and some of the changes that you might consider making in your life in order to lead on purpose.

1. Do I have a vision of a special future for the people who are important to me?

"Do not let your hearts be troubled. Believe in God, believe also in me. In my Father's house there are many dwelling places. If it were not so, would I have told you that I go to prepare a place for you? And if I go and prepare a place for you, I will come again, and will take you to myself, so that where I am, you may be also." (John 14:1-3)

As Jesus began preparing his disciples for life without him, he shared with them a vision of a special future that lay in store for them. He told them of a dwelling place—a mansion, if you will. This mansion would be the most incredible place they could ever imagine, and when they got there, they would find that their names had already been written on the mailbox in the front yard. Jesus himself would be there with them, and even though he had to leave them now, he would never leave them once they arrived to spend eternity with him. Jesus had a vision of a special future for those that were important to him.

Visions transform people. They present a picture of a special future that is captivating. I love Paul's vision of transformation: "Do not be conformed to this world, but be transformed by the renewing of your minds, so that you may discern what is the will of God—what is good and acceptable and perfect" (Romans 12:2).

In *The Gift of the Blessing* Gary Smalley and John Trent write: "Picturing a special future for a child, spouse, or friend can help bring out the best in their lives. It gives them a positive direction to strive toward and surrounds them with hope."[1] Later, describing parents speaking about a vision for their children's future, they write:

> Words that picture a special future for a child act like positive hormones that attach themselves to a child. In fact, they stimulate all kinds of positive feelings and decisions within a child that can help him or her grow. With words of a special future, a child can begin to work on a particular talent, have the confidence to try out for a school office, or even share his or her faith with other children.[2]

You can do the same for the people you serve. What vision has God given you of a special future for your congregation? What have you discerned is your role in the communication of that vision? Like a special hormone that attaches itself to people in your congregation, a vision of a special future can captivate the imaginations and the lives of those you serve. What could be more important than that?

When I speak to pastors or church leaders, I tell them that their primary purpose is to recognize that God has given them the members of their congregations as a *sacred trust* to develop and grow them into the people who God created them to be. That's leading on purpose in a nutshell. It's taking what God has created and providing opportunities for people to live out the purpose for which God has created them.

People with a vision of a special future change the world. They step out, even though it might be into the midst of conflict, and change their world, and in the end the world around them is blessed because of them. They don't do it for themselves, but for the sake of others. They start out with God's purpose, make the personal preparation necessary to communicate that purpose, and make a significant contribution by blessing the world around them.

Do I have a vision of a special future for the people who are important to me? How are you doing with this question? Circle the number that reflects where you are:

1   2   3   4   5   6   7   8   9   1 0
weak   strong

2. Do I live my life on purpose and with passion and intention according to God's plan?

I love the words of Jeremiah. I quote these words several times each year in sermons and teachings:

> For surely I know the plans I have for you, says the LORD, plans for your welfare and not for harm, to give you a future with hope. . . . When you search for me, you will find me; if you seek me with all your heart, I will let you find me, says the LORD. (Jeremiah 29:11, 13-14)

Can the will and plans of God be known for a person's life, or for the life of a congregation? If so, it's through a mirror dimly

(1 Corinthians 13:12). But with prayer and discernment we can come closer to the heart of God for our lives than if we never seek it.

I now know that I am closer to God's heart, to where God wants me to be, than ever before. That doesn't result in an over-confidence that "I'm right" when people disagree with me. In fact, it only gives a deeper humbleness, gentleness, and patience when faced with conflict.

When I was in college, I loved to play pinball. In those days you had to push a lever to get the ball up; you'd pull back the handle to launch the ball, and the excitement would begin. The ball would bounce back and forth, propelled quickly off the rubber bumpers, and eventually start to drain toward the bottom where it was hit by the flippers to be thrust again against the bumpers. Lights would flash accompanied by a variety of sounds, and the longer I could keep the ball in action, the more points I scored. After a while the ball would drop down the deep, dark pit at the bottom of the machine. The lever would be pushed, the handle pulled back, and the whole routine would start all over again.

Do you ever feel like life is like that?

I know that church life as a pastor or leader can sometimes feel that way. I know that Bob, mentioned in the Introduction, felt that way; people didn't know what they wanted from their church or from him, and nobody knew what God was calling them to do. Life can become an endless series of being batted around by bumpers, with lights flashing and sounds sparkling, until each day ends and you get up and do it all over again. There certainly needs to be a way to live life with more purpose and intention than that.

I hope and pray that some of this book will be a blessing to you as a pastor or leader in your congregation. I know that I have been blessed by learning and living with the principles set forth here. I know that for many years my life was like living a pinball game. But I also know that feeling Dennis had (chapter 1) when he said, "I know I'm doing what God wants me to be doing, and I'm having the time of my life." Dennis is a good friend, and I love and respect him. When I grow up, I want to be even more like him. He's discovered the secret of living on purpose and with passion and intention according to God's plan.

Do I live my life on purpose and with passion and intention according to God's plan? How are you doing with this question? Circle the number that reflects where you are:

1   2   3   4   5   6   7   8   9   1 0
weak   strong

3. Do I live my dream?

Little things die. People die. Dreams live.

What vision do you have that is bigger than you? What is the dream for which you are living your life? True significance comes from following a dream and living every day of your life toward that dream.

Listen to God's dream through Joel:

Then afterward I will pour out my spirit on all flesh; your sons and your daughters shall prophesy, your old men shall dream dreams, and your young men shall see visions. Even on the male and female slaves, in those days, I will pour out my spirit.
(Joel 2:28-29)

That's a dream by which to live. Even old men shall dream dreams, and young men shall see visions. Who can forget Dr. Martin Luther King Jr.'s dream about children being known for the content of their character more than the color of their skin? Little things die. People die. Dreams live.

Part of the reason for this book is to encourage you to capture the dream God has for your congregation and for your life. Dare to dream. Capture that dream, and live with it. Remember the words from Ephesians 3:20-21: "Now to him who by the power at work within us is able to accomplish abundantly far more than all we can ask or imagine, to him be glory in the church and in Christ Jesus to all generations, forever and ever. Amen."

You might even want to circle the words, "is able to accomplish abundantly far more than all we can ask or imagine." Ponder each of those words. I sometimes wonder if God laughs at the smallness of our dreams. What dream can you live that is far more than you can even ask or imagine?

Do I live my dream? How are you doing with living the dream God placed in your heart? Circle the number that reflects where you are:

1   2   3   4   5   6   7   8   9   10
weak   strong

4. Do I live for what will be on my tombstone?

Walk around a cemetery, and you'll find that tombstones give a testimony of the life that people lived. Think of what the following tombstone testimonies say:

He walked with God on earth, now he rests with God in heaven.

To our Dad and best friend; we all love you.

Beloved one and friend: On your way to God you left your mark.

Loved by her daughters, her grandchildren, and her husband;
Loving you and having you love me
has been the best thing in my life.

Sven: family man, fisherman, boat builder, inventor,
generous, honest, missed.

Consider the words of Jesus in the high priestly prayer, when he was making a summary statement of his life: "I glorified you on earth by finishing the work that you gave me to do" (John 17:4).

Consider the following exercise. What will be the summary of your life on your tombstone? Complete the sentences:

*(Your name)*_____ *accomplished many things in this life, including:*

But will be best remembered by those whose lives s/he touched for:

Ever since reading Tony Campolo's book, *Who Switched the Price Tags?*, I've been haunted by the sociological study that he quoted which asked 50 people over the age of 95 the question, "If you could live your life over again, what would you do differently?" Three answers dominated the results of the study. If they could live their lives over again, they would reflect more, risk more, and do more things that would live on after they were dead.[3]

Several chapters later he tells of a pastor who got up to deliver the closing words at their Student Recognition Day:

> "Children," he said, "you're going to die! You may not think you're going to die. But you're going to die. One of these days, they're going to take you out to the cemetery, drop you in a hole, throw some dirt on your face, and go back to the church and eat potato salad.
>
> "When you were born," he said, "you alone were crying and everybody else was happy. The important question I want to ask is this: When you die are you alone going to be happy, leaving everybody else crying? The answer depends on whether you live to get titles or you live to get testimonies. When they lay you in the ground, are people going to stand around reciting the fancy titles you earned, or are they going to stand around giving testimonies of the good things you did for them? . . . Titles are good

things to have. But if it ever comes down to a choice between a title or a testimony—go for the testimony."[4]

What are they going to say about you after you die, when they go to the cemetery and throw dirt on your face, and then go back to the church and eat potato salad and talk about you? Are you living for a title or a testimony? Are you in a position of leadership in your congregation because of status or personal influence, or do you really want to leave the testimony of a legacy for those who will come after you for generations?

Søren Kierkegaard wrote in his personal journal, "What I really lack is to be clear in my mind what I am to do, what I am to know. . . . The thing is to understand myself, and to see what God really wishes me to do . . . to find the idea for which I can live and die."[5]

Do I live for what will be on my tombstone? How are you doing with living your life in the way that you wish to be remembered? Circle the number that reflects where you are:

1   2   3   4   5   6   7   8   9   1 0
weak   strong

Live for a testimony of what God is doing in your life. Don't worry about the titles that you accumulate. Find that idea, that dream, that vision for which you can live, and passionately pursue it. Lead your congregation in ways that you can help them discover their gifts. Dream of opportunities with them, and provide for them the means by which they can glorify God by finishing the work God gave them to do.

There's nothing more important in this world than knowing Jesus. The most important dream of a pastor or leader is to bring people purposefully into a relationship with him. It's my hope and prayer that this book will give you encouragement and passion to pursue that dream.

Notes

Chapter 1 – The Purpose-Driven Phenomenon

1. Rick Warren, *The Purpose-Driven Church: Growth without Compromising Your Message and Mission* (Grand Rapids: Zondervan, 1995).

2. Ibid., 13.

3. Rick Warren, *The Purpose-Driven Life: What on Earth Am I Here For?* (Grand Rapids: Zondervan, 2002).

4. Warren, *The Purpose-Driven Church*, 103–9.

5. Ibid., 87.

6. William M. Easum, *Dancing with Dinosaurs: Ministry in a Hostile and Hurting World* (Nashville: Abingdon, 1993), 38–39.

7. Warren, *The Purpose-Driven Church*, 361–64.

Chapter 2 – Intentionality and Leading on Purpose

1. Lewis Carroll, *Alice's Adventures in Wonderland* (originally published 1864.)

2. *Lutheran Book of Worship* (Minneapolis: Augsburg; Philadelphia: Board of Publication, Lutheran Church in America, 1978), 121–25.

3. *Lutheran Book of Worship*, 201.

4. Eric W. Gritsch, *Fortress Introduction to Lutheranism* (Minneapolis: Fortress Press, 1994), 120.

5. Ibid., 104.

6. Cited in the November 2003 issue of *The Lutheran*.

7. SHAPE is more fully explained in chapter 3 and at www.leadingonpurpose.org.

8. Information on LifeKeys can be found at www.lifekeys.com.

Chapter 3 – Congregational Engagement: Getting the Order Right

1. For a wonderful exposition of Peter's walk on the water and Jesus' radical call to discipleship read John Ortberg, *If You Want to Walk on Water, You've Got to Get Out of the Boat* (Grand Rapids: Zondervan, 2001).

2. Michael Slaughter, *Unlearning Church: Just When You Thought You Had Leadership All Figured Out* (Loveland, Colo.: Group, 2002), 29.

3. Some of the statistics quoted here are from a Gallup "Summit on Congregational Engagement" held in Omaha, Nebraska, in November 2003. Other dates for similar summits are found at www.gallup.com.

4. Michael W. Foss, *Power Surge: Six Marks of Discipleship for a Changing Church* (Minneapolis: Fortress Press, 2000), 21.

5. Ibid., 21.

6. The SHAPE inventory is much more fully explained at www.leadingonpurpose.org. In Saddleback's structure it is the 301 Class on Spiritual Maturity.

7. This is a new resource available through the Gallup Organization. For more information visit www.gallup.com, or see the Bibliography in this book or the resources linked to chapter 3 at www.leadingonpurpose.org.

Chapter 4 – Ministry Teams

1. Kelly A. Fryer, *Reclaiming the "L" Word: Renewing the Church from Its Lutheran Core* (Lutheran Voices; Minneapolis: Augsburg Fortress, 2003), 77.

2. William M. Easum, *Sacred Cows Make Gourmet Burgers: Ministry Anytime Anywhere by Anyone* (Nashville: Abingdon, 1995), 119.

3. Michael W. Foss, *Power Surge: Six Marks of Discipleship for a Changing Church* (Minneapolis, Fortress Press, 2000), 144.

4. Just for clarification, the areas of financial and property administration and the area of youth ministry don't always fit neatly into this pattern. Some churches organize themselves around the five purposes, plus administration and youth. Other congregations fit administration under the Ministry purpose and youth under the Discipleship purpose. What's most important is to contextualize this model in your specific setting.

5. See chapter two, page 9, for a review of the Concentric Circles of Commitment.

6. Our cars ministry team was highlighted in the issue of *The Lutheran* (February 1999).

7. These resources are footnoted in chapter 2.

Chapter 5 – Preaching on Purpose

1. *Lutheran Book of Worship* (Minneapolis: Augsburg; Philadelphia: Board of Publication, Lutheran Church in America, 1978), 74, 94, 117 (author's emphasis).

2. Rick Warren covers material similar to this in his preaching workshops and in resources available at www.pastors.com. Rick Warren also has some very helpful suggestions in Part Four of *The Purpose-Driven Church: Growth without Compromising Your Message and Mission* (Grand Rapids: Zondervan, 1995).

3. Summarized from Rick Warren's preaching workshop material.

Chapter 6 – A Lutheran Reading of The Purpose-Driven Life

1. Rick Warren, *The Purpose-Driven Life: What on Earth Am I Here For?* (Zondervan: Grand Rapids, 2002).

2. Warren, *The Purpose-Driven Life*, 9.

Chapter 7 – Transitioning to Leading on Purpose

1. Peter L. Steinke, *Healthy Congregations: A Systems Approach* (Bethesda, Md.: Alban Institute, 1996).

2. Dan Southerland, *Transitioning: Leading Your Church through Change* (Grand Rapids: Zondervan, 2000), 112.

3. Several new membership covenants are available at www.leadingonpurpose.org.

4. John P. Kotter, *Leading Change* (Boston: Harvard Business School Press, 1996).

5. Southerland, *Transitioning*, 36.

6. Robert O. Quinn, *Deep Change: Discovering the Leader Within* (San Francisco: Jossey-Bass, 1996), 5.

7. Ibid.

Chapter 8 – Leading on Purpose: Visioning a Faithful Future for Those You Serve

1. Gary Smalley and John Trent, *The Gift of the Blessing* (exp. ed.; Nashville: Thomas Nelson, 1993), 86.

2. Ibid., 90.

3. Anthony Campolo, *Who Switched the Price Tags? A Search for Values in a Mixed-up World* (Waco, Tex.: Word, 1986), 29.

4. Ibid., 59.

5. Søren Kierkegaard, *A Kierkegaard Anthology,* ed. Robert Bretall (Princeton, N.J.: Princeton University Press, 1973), 4–5.

Bibliography

Primary Texts

Foss, Michael W. *Power Surge: Six Marks of Discipleship for a Changing Church.* Minneapolis: Fortress Press, 2000.

Fryer, Kelly A. *Reclaiming the "L" Word: Renewing the Church from Its Lutheran Core.* Lutheran Voices. Minneapolis: Augsburg Fortress, 2003.

Warren, Rick. *The Purpose-Driven Church: Growth without Compromising Your Message and Mission.* Grand Rapids: Zondervan, 1995.

Warren, Rick. *The Purpose-Driven Life: What on Earth Am I Here For?* Grand Rapids: Zondervan, 2002.

Congregational Engagement and the Discovery of Gifts

The Gallup Organization has a series of books that are meant to be read sequentially and are written for the business world, but the principles are directly applicable to congregational life. The fourth one is for faith-based communities.

Buckingham, Marcus, and Curt Coffman. *First, Break All the Rules: What the World's Greatest Managers Do Differently.* New York: Simon and Schuster, 1999.

Buckingham, Marcus, and Donald O. Clifton. *Now, Discover Your Strengths.* New York: Free Press, 2001.

Coffman, Curt, and Gabriel Gonzales-Molina. *Follow This Path: How the World's Greatest Organizations Drive Growth by Unleashing Human Potential.* New York: Warner, 2002.

Winseman, Albert L., Donald O. Clifton, and Curt Liesveld. *Living Your Strengths: Discover Your God-given Talents, and Inspire Your Congregation and Community.* Washington, D.C.: Gallup, 2003.

Other recommended resources include:

Foss, Michael W. *Real Faith for Real Life: Living the Six Marks of Discipleship.* Minneapolis: Augsburg Books. 2004.

Luther Seminary (St. Paul, Minnesota) has just started a major new initiative called Centered Life. It's not living a different life, but living life differently. Information is available at www.centeredlife.org.

Leading Congregational Transition and Change

Bandy, Thomas G. *Coaching Change: Breaking Down Resistance, Building Up Hope.* Nashville: Abingdon, 2000.

Easum, William M. *Sacred Cows Make Gourmet Burgers: Ministry Anytime Anywhere by Anyone.* Nashville: Abingdon, 1995.

Hunter, George C., III.. *Leading and Managing a Growing Church.* Nashville: Abingdon, 2000.

Kallestad, Walt. *Turn Your Church Inside Out: Building a Community for Others.* Minneapolis, Augsburg Fortress, 2001.

Kotter, John P. *Leading Change.* Boston: Harvard Business School Press, 1996.

There are several books based on Nehemiah and leadership, including:

Southerland, Dan. *Transitioning: Leading Your Church through Change.* Grand Rapids: Zondervan, 1999.

Stanley, Andy. *Visioneering: God's Blueprint for Developing and Maintaining Personal Vision.* Sisters, Ore.: Multnomah, 1999.

Swindoll, Charles R. *Hand Me Another Brick: How Effective Leaders Motivate Themselves and Others.* Nashville: Thomas Nelson, 1990.

Developing Ministry Teams

Cladis, George. *Leading the Team-Based Church: How Pastors and Church Staffs Can Grow Together into a Powerful Fellowship of Leaders.* San Francisco: Jossey-Bass, 1999.

Cordeiro, Wayne. *Doing Church as a Team.* Revised and expanded edition. Ventura, Calif.: Regal, 2001.

Maxwell, John C. *The Seventeen Indisputable Laws of Teamwork: Embrace Them and Empower Your Team.* Nashville: Thomas Nelson, 2001.

Congregational Leadership

Barna, George. *A Fish Out of Water: Nine Strategies Effective Leaders Use to Help You Get Back into the Flow.* Nashville: Integrity, 2002.

Easum, Bill. *Leadership on the Otherside: No Rules, Just Clues.* Nashville: Abingdon, 2000.

Hybels, Bill. *Courageous Leadership.* Grand Rapids: Zondervan, 2002.

Martoia, Ron. *Morph: The Texture of Leadership for Tomorrow's Church.* Loveland, Colo.: Group, 2003.

Maxwell, John C. *The Twenty-one Irrefutable Laws of Leadership: Follow Them and People Will Follow You.* Nashville: Thomas Nelson, 1998.

Slaughter, Michael. *Unlearning Church: Just When You Thought You Had Leadership All Figured Out.* Loveland, Colo.: Group, 2002.

Sweet, Leonard. *Aqua Church: Essential Leadership Arts for Piloting Your Church in Today's Fluid Culture.* Loveland, Colo.: Group, 1999.

Changing Church Culture

Easum, Bill, and Dave Travis. *Beyond the Box: Innovative Churches That Work.* Loveland, Colo.: Group, 2003.

Stanley, Andy, and Ed Young. *Can We Do That? Twenty-four Innovative Practices That Will Change the Way You Do Church.* West Monroe, La.: Howard, 2002.

Wagner, C. Peter. *Churchquake! How the New Apostolic Reformation Is Shaking Up the Church As We Know It.* Ventura, Calif.: Regal, 1999.

BV 652.1 .B865 2004
Burtness, Eric
Leading on Purpose.

DATE DUE

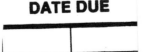